Henry Herbert Pembroke

Military Equitation

Or, a method of breaking horses, and teaching soldiers to ride. Designed for the use of the army.

Henry Herbert Pembroke

Military Equitation

Or, a method of breaking horses, and teaching soldiers to ride. Designed for the use of the army.

ISBN/EAN: 9783337307820

Printed in Europe, USA, Canada, Australia, Japan

Cover: Foto ©Paul-Georg Meister /pixelio.de

More available books at **www.hansebooks.com**

MILITARY EQUITATION:
OR,
A METHOD OF BREAKING HORSES,
AND
TEACHING SOLDIERS TO RIDE.

DESIGNED FOR THE USE OF THE ARMY.

BY
HENRY EARL OF PEMBROKE,
&c. &c. &c.

Scientia, & Patientia.

——— ——— Equitem docuere fub armis
Infultare folo, et greffus glomerare fuperbos.   VIRG.

Vis confili expers mole ruit fuâ.   HOR.

THE FOURTH EDITION,
WITH PLATES.

LONDON:
PRINTED FOR G. AND T. WILKIE, NO. 57, PATER-NOSTER-ROW;
AND
E. AND J. EASTON, SALISBURY.

MDCCXCIII.

TO
THE KING.

S I R,

WHEN the firſt regiment of light dragoons was raiſed under the command of my friend General GEORGE AUGUSTUS ELIOTT, we had frequent occaſion to lament together the wretched ſyſtem of HORSEMANSHIP, that at preſent prevails in the ARMY: A ſyſtem diſgraceful in itſelf, and productive in its conſequences of the moſt fatal evils: For troops in their own nature moſt excellent and brave have been frequently rendered inferior to leſs powerful ones, both in men and horſes, for want of proper inſtructions and intelligence in this Art. Theſe ſerious conſiderations (for indeed they are very much ſo) induced me to write down and make public the following Leſſons, calculated for the uſe of the Cavalry: They are ſuch as I have always practiſed

DEDICATION.

tifed myfelf; and taught both in the above-mentioned regiment and elfewhere, with conftant fuccefs. Incited by thefe reafons, I thus prefume to lay at your Majefty's feet this little work, the outlines only of a more extenfive, general one, which I intend to make public hereafter, fhould I find time to finifh it: And I am the more encouraged to it from the honour You have often done me of talking to me upon HORSEMANSHIP, as alfo from this confidence, that if what I here recommend, be deemed in any wife likely to be ufeful, (as I flatter myfelf it may, if candidly examined, and judicioufly practifed) it will not fail of receiving Your MAJESTY's Royal Approbation and Support. I am,

SIR,

Your MAJESTY's

MOST DUTIFUL SUBJECT,

AND DEVOTED SERVANT,

PEMBROKE.

PEMBROKE-HOUSE,
FEB. 15, 1761.

CONTENTS OF THE FOLLOWING TREATISE.

CHAP. I.

The method of preparing horses to be mounted, with the circumstances relative to it. - - - - page 1

CHAP. II.

The method of placing the men and rendering them firm on horseback, with some occasional instructions for them and the horses; and of bits. - - - page 6

CHAP. III.

The method of suppling horses with men upon them, by the Epaule *en dedans, &c. with and without a longe, on circles and on strait lines; and of working horses in hand.* - - - - - - - - page 31

CONTENTS.

CHAP. IV.

Of the head to the wall, and of the croupe to the wall. - - - - - - - - - page 53

CHAP. V.

The Trot. - - - - - - page 61

CHAP. VI.

The method of reining back---and of moving forwards immediately after---of piaffing---of pillars, &c.---of moving pillars, &c. - - - - - page 71

CHAP. VII.

The method of teaching horses to stand fire, noises, alarms, fights, &c.---of preventing their lying down in the water---to stand quiet to be shot off from---to go over rough and bad ground ---to leap hedges, gates, ditches, &c. standing and flying--- to disregard dead horses---to swim, &c. - - page 80

CHAP.

CONTENTS.

CHAP. VIII.

The method of curing restivenesses, vices, defences, starting, and stumbling, &c. - - - - - page 88

CHAP. IX.

Several remarks and hints on shoeing, feeding, management of horses, &c. &c. - - - - - page 97

ERRATA.

Page 42. l. 14. dele the *comma* after *properly*.
57. l. 15. for *appui's* read *appuis*.
61. l. 4. place a *comma* after *determine*.
69. l. 2. place a *colon* after *themselves*.
90. l. 11. place a *full stop* after *to*.
101. l. 15. for *detestible* read *detestable*.
103. l. 17. for *bevilled* read *bevelled*.
120. l. 17. dele *on* after *almost*.

A
METHOD
OF
BREAKING HORSES,
AND
TEACHING SOLDIERS TO RIDE, &c.

CHAP. I.

The method of preparing horses to be mounted, with the circumstances relative to it.

THOUGH all horses for the service are generally bought at an age, when they have already been backed, I would have them begun and prepared for the rider with the same care, gentleness and caution, as if they had never been handled or backed, in order to prevent accidents, which might else arise from skittishness or other caufes: and as it is proper, that they fhould be taught the figure of the ground they are to go upon, when they are at firft mounted, they fhould be previoufly trotted in a *longe* on large circles, without any one upon them; and without a faddle, or any thing elfe, at firft, which might hurt, conftrain, tickle, or make them any ways uneafy.

The manner of doing this is as follows: Put an eafy *caveffon* upon the horfe's nofe, and make him go forwards round you, ftanding quiet and holding the *longe*; and let another man, if you find it neceffary, follow him with a whip: All this muft be done very gently, and but a little at a time; for more horfes are fpoilt by over-much work, than by any other treatment whatever; and that by very contrary effects, for fometimes it drives them into vice, madnefs and defpair, and often it ftupifies them and totally difpirits them. An excellent way of *longing* horfes, who are apt to carry their heads low, (which many do) is to *longe* them with a cord buckled to the top of the head-ftall, and paffing from thence through the eye of the fnaffle into the hand of the perfon who holds the *longe*.

The

The firſt obedience required in a horſe, is going forwards: 'Till he performs this duty freely, never even think of making him rein back, which would inevitably render him reſtive: As ſoon as he goes forwards readily, ſtop and careſs him. You muſt remember in this, and likewiſe in every other exerciſe, to uſe him to go equally well, to the right and left; and when he obeys, careſs him and diſmiſs him immediately. A horſe, though ever ſo perfect to one hand only, is but a half dreſſed horſe. If a horſe, that is very young, takes fright and ſtands ſtill, lead on another horſe before him, which probably will induce him inſtantly to follow. Put a ſnaffle in his mouth; which ſnaffle ſhould be full, and thick in the mouth-piece, and not too ſhort: and when he goes freely, ſaddle him, girting him at firſt very looſe. Let the cord, which you hold, be long and looſe; but not ſo much ſo, as to endanger the horſe's entangling his legs in it. It muſt be obſerved, that ſmall circles, in the beginning, would conſtrain the horſe too much, and put him upon defending himſelf. No bend muſt be required at firſt: never ſuffer him to gallop falſe; but whenever he attempts it, ſtop him without delay, and then set him off afresh. If he gallops of his own accord, and true, permit him to continue it; but if he does it not voluntarily, do not demand it of him at first. Should he fly and jump, shake the cord gently upon his nose without jerking it, and he will fall into his trot again. If he stands still, plunges or rears, let the man, who holds the whip, make a noise with it; but never touch him, 'till it be absolutely necessary to make him go on. When you change hands, stop and caress him, and entice him by fair means to come up to you: for by presenting yourself, as some do, on a sudden before horses, and frightening them to the other side, you run a great risk of giving them a shyness. If he keeps his head too low, heighten your hand, and shake the *cavesson* to make him raise it: And in whatever the horse does, whether he walks, trots, or gallops, let it be a constant rule, that the motion be determined and really such as is intended, without the least shuffling, pacing, or any other irregular gait. A false gait should never be suffered. The trot is the pace, which enables all quadrupeds to balance and support themselves with firmness and ease. When he goes lightly, and freely,

tie

BREAKING HORSES, &c.

tie his head a little inwards by degrees: more, and more fo, as he grows more fupple, both in trotting, and galloping, in the *longe*, without any one upon him. Great care muft be taken, that he always goes true, and that his head is not kept tied for any time together; for if it was, he would infallibly get a trick of leaning on the rein, and throw himfelf heavily upon his fhoulders, when he grew tired. Every regiment fhould have fome covered place for their riding during the winter, or nothing hardly can be done in the bad feafon. In good weather, it is full as well, and more pleafant, to work out of doors: and indeed doing fo frequently prevents local routines, which horfes are fometimes particularly apt to take in fhut fchools, if great care is not taken. On the other hand, they are more often *diftraied*, and apt to lofe their attention by various objects, in fields, than they are in a riding-houfe. It is therefore difficult to decide, either for the one, or the other. There is more liberty in the one, than in the other, and horfes out of doors grow ufed to objects they would otherwife fear. In fhut fchools, work may be more exactly done, perhaps, and the ground there is beft. Both are good at proper feafons, and either will do very well, if the Riding-Mafter is good.

CHAP.

CHAP. II.

The method of placing the men, and rendering them firm on horseback; with some occasional instructions for them and the horses; and of bits.

'TIS necessary that the greatest attention, and the same gentleness, that is used in teaching the horses, be observed likewise in teaching the men, especially at the beginning. Every method and art must be practised to create and preserve, both in man and horse, all possible feeling and sensibility, contrary to the usage of most riding-masters, who seem industriously to labour at abolishing these principles both in the one and the other. As so many essential points depend upon the manner, in which a man is at first placed on horseback, it ought to be considered, and attended to with the strictest care and exactness.

The absurdity of putting a man, who perhaps has never before been upon a horse, (or if he has, 'tis probably so much the worse) on a rough trotting one, on which he is obliged (supposing the horse is insensible enough to suf-

fer

BREAKING HORSES, &c.

fer it; and if he be not, the man runs a great rifk of breaking his neck) to ftick with all the force of his arms and legs, is too obvious to need mentioning. This rough work, all at once, is plainly as detrimental at firft, as it is excellent afterwards in proper time. No man can be either well, or firmly feated on horfeback, unlefs he be mafter of the ballance of his body, quite unconftrained, with a full poffeffion of himfelf, and at his eafe, on all occafions whatever; none of which requifites can he enjoy, if his attention be otherwife engaged; as it muft wholly be in a raw, unfuppled, and unprepared lad, who is put at once upon a rough horfe: In fuch a diftrefsful ftate he is forced to keep himfelf on at any rate, by holding to the bridle, (at the expence of the fenfibility both of his own hand, and the horfe's mouth) and by clinging with his legs, in danger of his life, and to the certain depravation of a right feeling in the horfe;---a thing abfolutely neceffary to be kept delicate, for the forming properly both of man and horfe; not to mention the horrid appearance of fuch a figure, rendered totally incapable of ufe and action.

The firft time a man is put on horfeback, it ought to be

be upon a very gentle one. He never fhould be made to trot, 'till he is quite eafy in the walk, and then on very eafy horfes at firft. Afterwards, as he grows firmer, put him on rougher horfes, and augment by degrees the velocity of the trot. He fhould not gallop, 'till he can trot well; becaufe, though the motion of the gallop is the eafieft, a horfe may be more eafily unfettled in galloping than in trotting. The fame muft be obferved in regard to horfes: they fhould never be made to trot, 'till they are obedient, and their mouths are well formed on a walk; nor be made to gallop, 'till the fame be effected on a trot. When he is arrived at fuch a degree of firmnefs in his feat, the more he trots, (which no man whatever fhould ever leave off) and the more he rides rough horfes, the better. This is not only the beft method, (I may fay, the only right one) but alfo the eafieft and the fhorteft: by it, a man is foon made fufficiently an horfeman for a foldier; but by the other deteftable methods, that are commonly ufed, a man, inftead of improving, contracts all forts of bad habits, and rides worfe and worfe every day; the horfe too becomes daily more and more unfit for ufe. In proceeding according to the man-

ner

ner I have propofed, a man is rendered firm and eafy upon the horfe, and, as it were, of a piece with him; both his own and the horfe's fenfibility is preferved, and each in a fituation fit to receive and practife all leffons effectually: for if the man and horfe do not both work without difficulty and conftraint, the more they are exercifed, the worfe they become; every thing they do, is void of all grace, and of all ufe. When the man has acquired a perfect firmnefs on a faddle, he fhould by degrees be made equally firm on a rug, or on a horfe's bare back; fo much fo, as to be as firm, to work as well, and be quite as much at his eafe, as on any demi-pique faddle. Very little patience and attention will bring this about.

Among the various methods, that are ufed, of placing people on horfeback, few are directed by reafon. Some infift, that fcarce any preffure at all fhould be upon the backfide; others would have the feat be almoft upon the back-bone: out of thefe two contrary, and equally ridiculous methods, an excellent one may be found, by taking the medium. Before you let the man mount, teach him to know, and always to examine, if the curb be well placed,

placed; (I mean, when the horſe has a bit in his mouth, which at firſt he ſhould not, but only a ſnaffle, 'till the rider is firm in his ſeat, and the horſe alſo ſomewhat taught) and likewiſe if the noſe-band be properly tight; the throat-band looſiſh, and the mouth-piece neither too high, nor too low in the horſe's mouth, but rightly put, ſo as not to wrinkle the ſkin, nor to hang lax; the girts drawn moderately, but not too tight; the crupper, and the breaſt-plate, properly adjuſted, and whether the reins are of equal length. They ſhould be frequently taken off and made ſo, when they are found not to be ſo. A very good and careful hand may venture on a bit at firſt, and ſucceed with it full as well, as by beginning with a ſnaffle alone: but ſuch a proceeding will require more care, more delicacy, and more time, than can be expected in a corps, whoſe numbers are ſo confiderable, and where there are ſo few, if any good riders: A raw man is much eaſier taught to do well, than one, who has learnt ever ſo long, on bad principles; for it is much more difficult to undo, than to do; and the ſame in reſpect to the horſe. On colts, it is better in all ſchools whatſoever, to avoid any preſſure on the bars juſt at firſt, which a curb, though ever ſo deli-

cately

cately ufed, muft in fome degree occafion. Whoever begins a horfe with a bridle, muft be, in every refpect, a very good, delicate rider, and be very careful that the horfe does not get and keep his head low, whereby all action in the fhoulders is fpoiled. I have feen fome fchools, in France particularly, where a bit was immediately put into a horfe's mouth at firft; but I have conftantly obferved in thofe fchools, that their horfes carried their heads low, that the motion of their fhoulders was not free, but confined. Here and there one horfe or fo, indeed, there might be, whofe fore-hand nature had placed fo high, that nothing could bring it down low. Great care muft be taken to make the men ufe their fnaffles delicately; otherwife, as a fnaffle has not the power, which a bridle has upon a horfe's mouth, they will ufe themfelves to take fuch liberties with it, as will quite fpoil their hands, and teach the horfes to pull, be dead in hand, and quite upon their fhoulders, entirely deprived of good action. Whenever any bridles are ufed, (and they always fhould be at a proper time, when the horfes' heads are high, and they are well determined, light in hand, and free in their motions) they muft be all the fame; for though different mouths

mouths require different forts of bits, it is abfolutely necessary that fome general uniform fort fhould be ufed throughout a whole regiment. They fhould differ only in breadth, according to the breadth of each horfe's mouth. There needs no great variety of fizes for bitting a whole regiment. The beft I could ever pitch on, after repeated trials, is one made after the following drawing. *(Plate* 1.) The weight of the bit, without the curb, is about fourteen ounces three quarters, the curb alone weighs about four ounces and a quarter, and the little chain to prevent horfes taking the branches in their mouth, (which is a trick very many horfes get) three quarters of an ounce. The whole together weighs one pound, three ounces, and three quarters. The rings to the branches fhould be fixed, and the reins buckled to them, to prevent the latter from twifting. The mouth-piece is of a proper fhape, height, and fubftance, and is fixed. All fuch as are not fo, and move in the joint, have a bad, uncertain effect. Thin curbs are bad, and apt, if at all roughly ufed, (a thing very difficult to prevent at all times in fome people's hands) to cut, and damage the horfe's mouth very much. They fhould be flat, broad,

and

BREAKING HORSES, &c.

and eafy, that they may not hurt the horfe's *barbe*, but they muft not be thick, or heavy. This bridle is calculated for light troops. Heavier corps, who have larger horfes, and of another kind, may have the branches a quarter of an inch longer, and the whole bridle fomewhat, but very little more fubftantial. Bridles fhould never be ufed with raw recruits, or with raw horfes, at firft: a plain mouthed, fmooth fnaffle, does much better; the twifted, fharp, cutting ones, are barbarous, callous making inftruments at beft; the fingle ones, as well as the double rein ones, are often very ufeful, and agreeable even with dreffed horfes upon all airs whatfoever, if they are apt to get their heads low. When thefe neceffary precautions have been all taken, let the man approach the horfe gently near the fhoulder; then taking the reins and an handful of the mane in his left hand, let him put his left foot foftly into the left ftirrup, (but not too far in) by pulling it towards him, left he touch the horfe with his toe, which might frighten him; then raifing himfelf up, let him reft a moment on it with his body upright, but not ftiff: and after that, paffing his right leg clear over the faddle, without rubbing againft any thing, let him feat

himfelf

himself gently down. The same precautions must also be taken in dismounting. He must be cautious not to take the reins too short, for fear of making the horse rear, run, or fall back, or throw up his head; but let him hold them of an equal length, neither tight nor slack, and with the little finger betwixt them. 'Tis fit that horses should be accustomed to stand still to be mounted, and not stir 'till the rider pleases. The man, who holds the horse to be mounted, must not do it by the bridle, but only by the cheeks of the head-stall, and gently, otherwise the same inconvenience might arise, as from the rider's holding the reins too short himself in mounting. All soldiers should be instructed to mount and dismount equally well on both sides, which may be of very great use in times of hurry and confusion. Place the man in his saddle, with his body rather back, and his head held up with ease, without stiffness; seated neither forwards, nor very backwards, with the breast pushed out a little, and the lower part of the body likewise a little forwards; the thighs and legs turned in without constraint, and the feet in a strait line, neither turned in nor out: By this position, the natural weight of the thighs has a proper and sufficient pressure of itself,

self, and the legs are in readiness to act, when called upon: they must hang down easy and naturally, and be so placed, as not to be wriggling about, touching and tickling the horse's sides, but always near them in case they should be wanted, as well as the heels.

The body must be carefully kept easy and firm, and without any rocking, when in motion; which is a bad habit very easily contracted, especially in galloping. The left elbow must be gently leant against the body, a little forwards; unless it be so rested, the hand cannot be steady, but will be always checking, and consequently have pernicious effects on the horse's mouth: and the hand ought to be of equal height with the elbow; if it were lower, it would constrain and confine the motion of the horse's shoulders, which must be free. I speak here of the position of the hand in general; for as the mouths of horses are different, the place of the hand also must occasionally differ: a leaning, low, heavy fore-hand, requires a high hand; and a horse that pokes out his nose, a low one. The right hand arm must be placed in symmetry with the left; only let the right hand be a little forwarder

warder or backwarder, higher or lower, as occasions may require: in order that both hands may be free, both arms must be a little bent at the elbow, to prevent stiffness.

A soldier's right hand should be kept unemployed in riding; it carries the sword, which is a sufficient business for it: In learning therefore to ride, the men should have a whip or switch in it, and hold it upwards, that they may thereby know how to carry their swords properly, keeping it downwards only, when they mount or dismount, that the horse may not be frightened at the sight of it.

The hand must be kept clear of the body, about two inches and a half forwards from it, with the nails turned opposite to the waistcoat buttons, and the wrist a little rounded with ease; a position not less graceful than ready for slackening, tightening, and moving the reins from one side to the other, as may be found necessary.

A firm and well balanced position of the body, on horseback, is (as has already been said) of the utmost consequence; as it affects the horse in every motion, and

in

BREAKING HORSES, &c.

is the best of helps: whereas on the contrary, the want of it is the greatest detriment to him, and an impediment in all his actions. Many people make a great difference about saddles, as a serious object of firmness; but nobody can be truly said to have a seat, who is not equally firm on flat, or demi-piqued saddles, on the true principles of equilibre, and ease. When the men are well placed, the more rough trotting they have, without stirrups, the better; but with a strict care always, that their position be preserved very exactly. As for those unfeeling fellows, who continue sticking by their hands, in spite of all the teacher's attention to prevent it, nothing remains to be done, but to make them drop the reins quite on a safe-going horse, and to keep their hands in the same position, as if they held them. In all cases without exception, but more especially in this, great care must be taken to hinder their clinging with their legs: in short, no sticking by hands or legs is ever to be allowed of at any time. If the motion of the horse be too rough, slacken it, 'till the rider grows by degrees more firm: and when he is quite firm and easy on his horse in every kind of motion, stirrups may be given him; but he must never leave off trotting often, and working often without any.

The stirrups must be neither short nor long; but of such a length that when the rider, being well placed, puts his feet into them, (about one-third of the length of the foot from the point of it) the points may be between two and three inches higher than the heels: longer stirrups are bad, and would make it very difficult for the rider to get his leg over the baggage, forage, cloak, &c. which are fastened on behind upon the saddle: and shorter would be bad in every respect, and answer no end at all. The length I mentioned above, is just the right one, and is to be taken in the following method: make the rider place himself upon the saddle, even, upright and well, with his legs hanging down, and the stirrups likewise: and when he is in this position, raise the rider's toe to an equal height with his heel, and take up the stirrup, 'till the bottom of it comes just under the ankle-bone. The stirrups must be exactly of an equal length. The rider must not bear upon his stirrups, but only let the natural weight of his legs rest on them: for if he bore upon them, he would be raised above, and out of his saddle; which should never be, except in charging sword in hand, with the body inclined forwards at the very instant of attacking.

ing. Spurs may be given, as foon as the rider is grown familiar with ftirrups, or even long before, if his legs are well placed.

Delicacy in the ufe of the hands, as well as in the ufe of the legs, may be given by the teacher to a certain degree; but 'tis nature alone that can beftow that great fenfibility, without which neither one nor the other can be formed to any great perfection. A hand fhould be firm, but delicate: a horfe's mouth fhould never be furprifed by any fudden tranfition of it, either from flack to tight, or from tight to flack. Every thing in horfemanfhip muft be effected by degrees, and with delicacy, but at the fame time with fpirit and refolution. That hand, which by giving and taking properly, gains its point with the leaft force, is the beft; and the horfe's mouth, under this fame hand's directions, will alfo confequently be the beft, fuppofing equal advantages in both from nature. This principle of gentlenefs fhould be obferved upon all occafions in every branch of horfemanfhip. Hard, bad mouths, may appear foft and good to an infenfible hand; fo that it is impoffible to form any judgment of a horfe's mouth by what any body tells you of it, unlefs you know the degree of fenfibility, and fcience that perfon is poffeffed of in horfemanfhip, or ride the horfe yourfelf. Sometimes the right hand may be neceffary, for a moment, upon fome troublefome horfes, to affift the left; but the feldomer this is done, the better; efpecially in a foldier, who has a fword to carry, and to make ufe of.

 The fnaffle muft on all occafions be uppermoft, that is to fay, the reins of it muft be above thofe of the bridle, whether the fnaffle or the bit be ufed feparately, or whether they be both ufed together. When the rider knows enough, and the horfe is fufficiently prepared and fettled to begin any work towards fuppling, one rein muft be fhortened according to the fide worked to, (as is explained in its proper place) but it muft never be fo much fhortened, as to make the whole ftrength reft on that rein alone; for, not to mention that the work would be falfe and bad, one fide of the horfe's mouth would by that means be always deadened; whereas on the contrary, it fhould always be kept frefh by its own play, and by the help of the oppofite rein's acting delicately in a fmaller

degree

degree of tenſion; the joint effects of which produce in a horſe's mouth the proper, gentle, and eaſy degree of *appui* or bearing; to preſerve which, when obtained, the horſe muſt not be over-worked; if he is, he will, beſides other bad conſequences, throw himſelf on his ſhoulders into the rider's hand, like a tired poſt-horſe on the road. Colts indeed, as well as men, at firſt muſt be taught the effect of the reins taken ſeparately, for fear of confounding them in the beginning with mixed effects of them at once. Avoid working in deep, bad ground; beſides its ſpoiling a horſe's paces, it obliges him to throw himſelf on his ſhoulders upon the rider's hand, and teaches him to toſs his head about diſagreeably.

A coward and a madman make alike bad riders, and are both alike diſcovered and confounded by the ſuperior ſenſe of the creature they are mounted upon, who is equally ſpoilt by both, though in very different ways. The coward, by ſuffering the animal to have his own way, not only confirms him in his bad habits, but creates new ones in him: and the madman, by falſe and violent motions and corrections, ruins the horſe, and drives him,

through

through defpair, into every bad and vicious trick that rage can fuggeft.

All horfes heads muft be kept very high, 'till they are quite determined, and free in the motions of their fhoulders.

It is very requifite in horfemanfhip, that the hand and legs fhould act in correfpondence with each other in every thing; the latter always fubfervient and affiftant to the former. Upon circles, in walking, trotting, or galloping, (I mean only where nothing more is intended) the outward leg is the only one to be ufed, and that only for a moment at a time, in order to make the horfe go true, if he be falfe; and as foon as that is done, it muft be taken away again immediately. If the horfe is lazy, or any ways retains himfelf, both legs muft be ufed, and preffed to his fides at the fame time together; if after having tried fofter methods, fuch as a gentle preffure of the thighs, and putting the legs back, they fhould fail, but not before. The lefs the legs are ufed in general, the better. Very delicate riders, in regular well attended good fchools, never want their help; and horfes fo dreffed,

BREAKING HORSES, &c.

fed, are by far superior to all others: they obey the smallest touch on the rein, or the least weight of the body thrown one way, or the other, imperceptibly, as may be necessary: the horse and man seem one, and the same, and such is the practice and teaching of great masters; but that perfection in the feeling of either man, or horse, is not to be expected in the hurry which can not be avoided in a regimental school, where the numbers are so great. By the term outward, is understood the side which is more remote from the center; and by inward, is meant the side next to the center. In reining back, the rider should be careful not to use his legs, unless the horse backs on his shoulders; in which case, they must be both applied gently at the same time, and correspond with the hand. If the horse refuse to back at all, the rider's legs must be gently approached, 'till the horse lifts up a leg, as if to go forwards; at which time, when that leg is in the air, the rein of the same side with that leg, which is lifted up, will easily bring that same leg backwards, and accordingly oblige the horse to back: but if the horse offers to rear, the legs must be instantly removed away. The inward rein must be the tighter on circles, so that the horse may bend and look inwards; and the outward one crossed over a little towards it; and both held in the left hand, that soldiers may not have their right employed, which, as has before been observed, must be left free for other more necessary uses.

Let the man and horse begin all lessons whatsoever on very slow motions, that they may have time to understand, and reflect on what is taught them; but though the motions are slow, they must not be dull, but determined, and without hesitation. In proportion as the effects of the reins are better comprehended, and the manner of working becomes more familiar, the quickness of motion must be increased. Every rider must learn to feel, without the help of the eye, when a horse goes false, even in the most speedy, and most violent motions, and remedy the fault accordingly: this is an intelligence, which nothing but practice, application, and attention, can give, in the beginning on slow motions. A horse may not only gallop false, but also trot and walk false. If a horse gallops false, that is to say, if going to the right, he leads with the left leg; or if going to the left, he leads with the
right;

right; or in cafe he is difunited, by which is meant, if he leads with the oppofite leg behind to that which he leads with before, ftop him immediately, and put him off again properly: the method of effecting this, is by approaching your outward leg, gently, and putting your hand outwards, ftill keeping the inward rein the fhorter, and the horfe's head inwards, if poffible; but if he fhould ftill refift, then bend and pull his head outwards alfo. Replace it again, bent properly inwards, the moment he goes off true. The help of the leg in this, and indeed all other cafes, muft not be made ufe of at all, 'till that of the hand alone has proved ineffectual. A horfe is faid to be difunited to the right, when going to the right, and confequently leading with the right leg before, he leads with the left behind; and is faid to be difunited to the left, when going to the left, and confequently leading with the left leg before, he leads with the right behind. A horfe may at the fame time be both falfe and difunited; in correcting both which faults, the fame method muft be ufed. He is both falfe and difunited to the right, when in going to the right he leads with the left leg before, and the right behind; notwithftanding that hinder leg be with propriety more forward under his belly, than the left, becaufe the horfe is working to the right: and he is falfe and difunited to the left, when in going to the left, he leads with the right leg before, and the left behind; notwithftanding, as above, that hinder leg be with propriety more forward under his belly than the right, becaufe the horfe is working to the left.

Care muft be taken, that horfes, in ftopping on the gallop, ftop true, behind particularly, which they are very apt not to do; efpecially in the longe, and bent, without any one on them.

In teaching men a right feat on horfeback, the greateft attention muft be given to prevent ftiffnefs, and fticking by force in any manner upon any occafion: ftiffnefs difgraces every work; and fticking ferves only to throw a man (when difplaced) a great diftance from his horfe, by the fpring he muft go off with: whereas by a proper equilibrating pofition of the body, and by the natural weight only of the thighs, he cannot but be firm, and fecure in his feat.

As

As the men become more firm, and the horses more supple, 'tis proper to make the circles less, but not too much so, for fear of throwing the horses forwards upon their shoulders.

No bits should be used, 'till the riders are firm, and the horses bend well to right and left; and then too always with the greatest care and gentleness. The silly custom of using strong and heavy bits, is in all good schools with reason laid aside, as it should be likewise in military riding: they pull down the horse's head, keep it low, thereby obstruct the action of the fore parts, and harden as much the hand of the rider, as the mouth of the horse; both which becoming every day more and more insensible together, nothing can be expected but a most unfeeling callousness both in one and the other. Some horses, when first the bit is put into their mouths, if great care be not taken, will put their heads very low; which low position of the head, provided the top of the head, and the nose, be nearly perpendicular, some ignorant people call a good one; without considering, that the higher the top of the head is, provided that it is nearly perpendicular with the nose, the better the position is on every account. If the top of the head is low, the position is a bad one, notwithstanding the head and nose being nearly perpendicular, because it obstructs the action of the fore parts. With such horses, raise your right hand with the *bridoon* in it, and play at the same time with the bit in the left hand, giving and taking. A strong bit, indeed, will flatter an ignorant hand, just at first; but it will never any other, nor even an ignorant one for any time together; for the horse's mouth will soon grow callous to it, and unfeeling, and the hand the same. Most horses, whose heads are heavy, are apt to stumble.

On circles, the rider must lean his body inwards; unless great attention be given to make him do it, he will be perpetually losing his seat outwards, every rapid or irregular motion the horse may make. 'Tis scarce possible for him to be displaced, if he leans his body properly inwards.

Instructions, both to man and horse, in riding, are of the greatest importance and consequence; as the success of actions in a great measure depends upon them. Squadrons

drons are frequently broken and defeated through the ignorance of the riders, or horses, but most commonly of both together. Many and various are the disasters, that arise from the horses not being properly prepared and suppled, and from the men not being taught firm seats, independent of their hands, and the mouths of their horses. Were the men rightly instructed how to keep the mouths of their horses fresh and obedient, and thereby maintain a cadenced pace, (be it ever so fast, or ever so slow) ranks would of course be always dressed, and unshaken, and consequently always powerful. The stoutest, and by nature, the best of cavalry, is often broken, and thereby rendered inferior far to much weaker and less respectable bodies than themselves, for want of being properly informed in the above-mentioned, and such-like particulars. This is a matter worthy of a serious inspection, consideration, and amendment, the neglect of which has upon many occasions been very fatal. 'Tis to be hoped, that some person of sufficient authority and knowledge will contrive to introduce many alterations, that appear very necessary in the cavalry. To what purpose is cavalry loaded with such monstrous heavy boots and firelock? a lighter,

yet

yet full as ſtrong, and much more ſerviceable boot might be eaſily contrived. A light carabine would ſuit them far better. A hat ſeems to me a ſilly and uſeleſs piece of dreſs in a ſoldier: it is continually falling off, eſpecially in action; nor can it ever ſerve as a protection againſt blows, &c. or bad weather, which are circumſtances of great conſequence: whereas a cap has no inconveniences at all attending it, may be made very ornamental and of a martial appearance, and in ſuch a manner, as to be a good fence againſt blows, rain, ſnow, and ſtormy winds, and alſo convenient to ſleep in.

CHAP. III.

The method of suppling horses, with men upon them, by the Epaule *en dedans, &c. with and without a longe, on circles and on strait lines; and of working horses in hand.*

WHEN a horse is well prepared and settled in all his motions, ('till when nothing more must be attempted) and the rider firm, (which is also as absolutely necessary) it will be proper then to proceed on towards a farther suppling and teaching of both. In regiments, especially those that are young, there are but very few, if any, tolerable horsemen; which makes the greatest exactness and gentleness absolutely necessary in the instructing of both: and more particularly so in this case, as horse and man are both ignorant, and must be both alike taught together; which is a difficulty, that does not exist in schools; for there a young rider is put upon a made, or at least a quiet horse; nor do any, but able riders, ever mount a raw one.

In setting out upon this new work, before which the horse should be taught to go well into the corners, both with his fore and hinder parts, on a walk, (without being bent, for that cannot be yet expected, though it will be soon) and be very light in hand; when he does it, begin by bringing the horse's head a little more inwards than before, pulling the inward rein gently to you by degrees. When this is done, try to gain a little on the shoulders, by keeping the inward rein the shorter, as before, and the outward one crossed over towards the inward one. The intention of these operations is this: the inward rein serves to bring in the head, and procures the bend; whilst the outward one, that is a little crossed, tends to make that bend perpendicular, and as it should be; that is to say, to reduce the nose and the forehead to be in a perpendicular line with each other: it also serves, if put forwards, as well as also crossed, to put the horse forwards, if found necessary; which is often requisite, many horses being apt in this, and other works, rather to lose their ground backwards, than otherwise, when they should rather advance: if the nose were drawn in towards the breast beyond the perpendicular, it would confine the motion

tion of the shoulders, and have other bad effects. All other bends, besides what I have above specified, are false. The outward rein, being crossed, not in a forward sense, but rather a little backwards, serves also, when necessary, to prevent the outward shoulder from getting too forwards, which facilitates the inward leg's crossing it; which is the motion that so admirably supples the shoulders. Care must be taken, that the inward leg pass over the outward one, without touching it; this inward leg's crossing over must be helped by the inward rein, which you must cross towards and over the outward rein, every time the outward leg comes to the ground, in order to lift and help the inward leg over it: at any other time, but just when the outward leg is come to the ground, it would be wrong to cross the inward rein, or to attempt to lift up the inward leg by it: nay, it would be demanding an absolute impossibility, and lugging about the reins and horse to no purpose; because a very great part of the horse's weight resting upon the inward leg would render such an attempt, not only fruitless, but also prejudicial to the sensibility of the mouth, and probably oblige him to defend himself, without being productive of any suppling motion whatsoever.

When the horse is thus far familiarly accustomed to what you have required of him, (but by no means before he is entirely so) then proceed to effect by degrees the same crossing in his hinder legs. By bringing in the fore legs more, you will of course engage the hinder ones in the same work: if they resist, the rider must bring both reins more inwards; and, if necessary, put back also, and approach his inward leg to the horse: and if the horse throws out his croup too far, the rider must bring both reins outwards, and if absolutely necessary, (but not otherwise) he must also delicately make use of his outward leg for a moment, in order to replace the horse properly; observing, that the croup should always be considerably behind the shoulders, which in all actions must go first; and the moment that the horse obeys, the rider must put his hand and leg again into their usual position. In this lesson, as indeed in almost all others, the corners must not be neglected: the horse should go well, and thoroughly into them. Bring his fore parts into them, by

crossing

BREAKING HORSES, &c.

crossing over the inward rein towards the outward one, (but without taking off from the proper bend of the head, neck, and shoulders) and bring them out of the corner again by crossing over the outward rein towards the inward one. These uses of the reins have also their proper effects upon the hinder parts.

Nothing is more ungraceful in itself, more detrimental to a man's seat, or more destructive of the sensibility of a horse's sides, than a continual wriggling unsettledness in a horseman's legs, which prevents the horse from ever going a moment together true, steady, or determined. 'Tis impossible, upon the whole, for a man to be too firm, settled, and gentle. A soft motion may be always inforced, if necessary, with ease; but an harsh one is irrecoverable, and its bad consequences very often almost irreparable. Men are very apt to get this trick of wriggling their legs, even in going strait forward, and more so with one leg particularly put back in changing of hands; which should be done by the reins only, in a graceful, still manner, and without letting the horse either throw himself over too fast, or go lazily over to the other hand;

the rider's hand alone is almost always sufficient; and, if it should not, many things should be tried, before so ugly, and bad a resource, as the above-mentioned is thought of; 1st, that of squeezing the thighs; 2d, approaching gently the calves of the legs, and 3d, using the spur; but without distorting the leg, or foot, which a good master will not permit to be done.

A horse should never be turned, without first moving a step forwards; an imperceptible motion only of the hand, from one side to the other, is sufficient to turn him. It must also be a constant rule, never to suffer a horse to be stopped, mounted, or dismounted, but when he is well placed.

At first, the figures worked upon must be great, and afterwards made less by degrees, according to the improvement which the man and horse make; and the cadenced pace also, which they work in, must be accordingly augmented. The changes from one side to the other, must be in a bold, determined trot, and at first quite straight forwards, without demanding any side motion on two *pistes*, which it is very necessary to require afterwards, when

BREAKING HORSES, &c.

when the horse is sufficiently suppled. By two *pistes* is meant, when the fore parts and hinder parts do not follow, but describe two different lines.

In the beginning, a *longe* is useful on circles, and also on straight lines, to help both the rider and the horse; but afterwards, when they are grown more intelligent, they should go alone. No one, not even the best riders, should ever quite leave off trotting every now and then, in the *longe*, both with, and without stirrups. At the end of the lesson rein back, and then put the horse, by a little at a time, forwards, by approaching both legs gently, and with an equal degree of pressure, to his sides, (if necessary) and playing with the bridle: if he rears, push him out immediately into a full trot. Shaking the *cavesson* on the horse's nose, and also putting one's self before him, and rather near to him, will generally make him back, though he otherwise refuse to do it: and moreover, a slight use and approaching of the rider's legs, will sometimes be necessary in backing, in order to prevent the horse from doing it too much upon his shoulders; but the pressure of the legs ought to be very small, and taken

quite

quite away the moment that he puts himself enough upon his haunches. The horse must learn by degrees to back upon a straight line, but to make him do so, the rider must not be permitted to have recourse immediately to his leg, and so distort himself by it, (which is generally practised with the common sort of riding-masters) but first try, if crossing over his hand and reins, to which ever side may be necessary, will not be alone sufficient; which most frequently it will; if not, then employ the leg, which should never be used 'till the last extremity.

After a horse is well prepared, and settled, and goes freely on in all his several paces, he ought to be in all his works kept, to a proper degree, upon his haunches, with his hinder legs well placed under him; whereby he will be always pleasant to himself, and his rider, will be light in hand, and ready to execute whatever may be demanded of him in reason, with facility, vigour, quickness, and delicacy.

The common method, that is used, of forcing a horse sideways, is a most glaring absurdity, and very hurtful to the animal in its consequences; for, instead of suppling

pling him, it obliges him to stiffen and defend himself, and often makes a creature, that is naturally benevolent, a restive, frightened, and vicious man-hater for ever. In general 'tis a maxim, as constantly to be remembered, as it is true, that it is more difficult to correct faults and bad habits, than to foresee and prevent them. Horses under riders, who use their legs, are, when going to work on two pistes, perpetually setting off with the croup foremost, than which nothing hardly can be worse. It is owing to the leg of the rider being applied to the side of the horse, before the hand has determined the fore parts of the animal, on the line, upon which he is to go.

For horses, who have very long and high fore-hands, and who poke out their noses, a running snaffle is of excellent use; but for such, as bore and keep their heads low, a common one is preferable; though any horse's head indeed may be kept up also with a running one, by the rider's keeping his hands very high and forwards; but that occasions a bad and aukward position in the man. They are, as plainly appears from their construction, bad for tripping and stumbling horses. Whenever either is

used

ufed alone, without a bridle, upon horfes that carry their heads low, and that bore, it muft be gently fawed about from one fide to the other.

Every body knows the conftruction of a running fnaffle. *(Plate 2.)* They will fee from that conftruction, that the purchafe of it is greater than that of a common one. As its firft point of *appui* is at the pommel of the faddle, lower than the rider's hand, they will alfo eafily perceive, why they are good for horfes, who have high light fore-hands, and why they are bad for fuch as have low and heavy ones. They are good for many horfes, when ufed as a bridoon with a bridle, in cafes of remarkably long, high fore-hands, and poking heads. On horfes, whofe heads and fore-hands are difficult to raife, a running fnaffle, but not one fixed in the ufual manner, is often very ufeful. The reins of it fhould be paffed through an eye fixed on each fide the head, pretty high up on the head-ftall towards the ears, before they come into the rider's hand. *(Plate 3.)* When fixed at firft to the rings on the head-ftall, and coming through the eyes of the fnaffle into the rider's hand, without being at all fixed to the faddle, they will

BREAKING HORSES, &c.

will often alfo be very ufeful. This leffon of the *Epaule en dedans*, is a very touchftone in horfemanſhip, both for man and horfe. Neither one nor the other can be dreffed to any degree without a confummate knowledge of it; but it muft not on any account be practifed in the field in exercifes, or evolutions: there the horfes muft always bend towards the fide they are going, a thing (to the fhame of the cavalry be it fpoken) fo rare to be feen. The *Epaule en dedans* reverfed, is particularly advantageous to horfes who are apt to throw themfelves forward. By reverfed, I mean when the fhoulders are worked upon the outward larger circle, and the croup on the fmaller circle next the center.

Horfes well perfected in the *Epaule en dedans* may undertake, and foon learn any other leffons whatfoever. It ought, like all others, to be practifed on all figures, circles, ftrait lines, fquares, &c. and when on this laft, which is an excellent leffon, (as alfo in every leffon, and on all figures, where there are corners and angles) care muft be taken concerning the fhoulders and croup, that, which ever of them is to enter the corner firft, may go quite into it; and let that which goes in laſt, follow exactly the ſame ground. This rule can not be too much attended to. The croup, indeed, can never enter the corner firſt, except in working backwards.

Of working in hand.

WORKING in hand requires a certain degree of activity, a quick eye, and, like every thing elſe about horſes, good temper, and judgment. Though it can not be looked upon as a very difficult thing, I have ſeen few people ſucceed in it: none indeed, to any conſiderable degree, except Sir SIDNEY MEDOWS, and the Cavaliere ROSSERMINI, at Piſa, author of the *Cavallo Perfetto*. Begin by trotting, then galloping the horſe properly, bent inwards by a ſtrap tied from the ſide ring on the *caveſſon* to the ring on the pad. *(Plate* 4.*)* To the head-ſtall of the longe, a ſtrap and buckle under the throat is very uſeful to prevent the ſide part of it from chafing againſt the eye, which it is very apt to do, when the bending ſtrap is uſed, and drawn at all tight. Do this for a little while

while only at a time. If the horse leans on the strap which is tied to bend him, take off the *cavesson*, and use in its stead one of the long strings which will be mentioned and explained a little further on, coming first from the ring on the pad, and from thence through the eye of the snaffle; *(Plate 5.)* and also, if the horse's head is low, through the ring on the head-stall, and from thence through the ring on the pad, *(Plate 6.)* into the hand of the person on foot, who must humour it, yielding and taking it up occasionally, which will prevent the horse's leaning, and make him light. *(Plate 6:)* The long string, thus used, will do very well alone, without the strap, when the horse is accustomed to bend, and to trot determined round the person who stands in the center, and holds the long string. After horses have been a little accustomed to be bent with a strap at the longe, they will very soon longe themselves, as it were; that is to say, that bent with the strap, they will go very well without any longe; and indeed, horses may be brought, with patience and gentleness, to work very well so on almost all lessons in hand. Next begin the *epaule en dedans*, and after that, the head to the wall, the croup to the wall, piaffing, backing, &c. on all figures, by degrees. I have observed, that most horses generally go the head to the wall more cordially at first,

firſt, than they do the croup to the wall. Working in hand is, if I may be allowed the expreſſion, a kind of driving. In explaining the method of working in hand, we will uſe the right all the way through. Two people on foot ſhould be employed about it; one indeed may do, and well, if it is a handy perſon, but two are much better at firſt: one of theſe people holds a long ſtring, and in ſome leſſons two long ſtrings, fixed, as ſhall be preſently explained, and a *chambriere*, ſtanding at ſome diſtance from the horſe: the other perſon ſtands near the horſe, holding the reins of the ſnaffle, and a hand whip, to keep the horſe off from him, when neceſſary. Girt a pad, with a crupper to it, upon the horſe: the pad muſt have a large ring in the center upon the top of it, and, about four inches lower down on each ſide, a ſmaller one. On the top of the pad, a little forwarder than the great ring, there muſt be a ſmall ſtrap, and buckle, which ſerve to buckle in the ſnaffle reins, and to prevent their floating about, and the horſe entangling his legs in them, in the longe. Horſes muſt never be worked in hand with any thing in their mouths, but a large, thick, plain, running ſnaffle: a bridle is too tickliſh, and would ſpoil the horſe's mouth, unleſs it be in the hands of a very able maſter indeed; for, in working in hand, it is next to impoſſible

to

BREAKING HORSES, &c.

to be sufficiently gentle, and delicate with it. The eyes of the snaffle should be large, and on the head-stall, about the height of the horse's eye, should be fixed a ring on each side. The person with the *chambriere* holds a long string, about eighteen feet long, (so as to be out of the reach of the horse's heels) which must be smooth, of a proper thickness, and not stick, but run free. This string, in the *epaule en dedans*, *(Plate* 7.) to the right, is buckled to the right hand small ring on the pad, where the reins of the running snaffle are first fixed; from thence it passes through the right eye of the snaffle, and from that to the right hand small ring on the head-stall, and through the large ring on the top of the pad, into the hand of the person who holds the *chambriere*, and who, by means of this string, bends the horse to the right, and brings in his shoulder; following him on his right side, and tightening and loosening the string, as he finds it necessary. If the horse's fore-hand is high, and well placed, it will not be necessary to pass the string through the ring upon the head-stall: at the same time, another person standing near the horse, the snaffle reins separated, and the right one tied loose on the right side, leads him on with the left rein of the snaffle in his hand, walking near

his

his head, and taking care to keep the shoulders in their proper place, and not to take off from the bend to the right, which is occasioned by the string in the other person's hand, who will find it most convenient, when working on this lesson to the right, to hold the string in his right hand, and the *chambriere* in his left, and so *vice versâ*. These he must make use of, and keep himself more or less upon the flank, center, or rear of the horse, as he finds necessary. In the changes from right to left, in the *epaule en dedans*, the person nearest the horse must be quick in getting on the horse's left side; and the person with the *chambriere* must do the same; the former coming round by the horse's head before him, and the latter round by his croup behind him; and so *vice versâ* to the left. In the head, and in the croup, to the wall, both the men are already properly placed for the changes. In this lesson of the *epaule en dedans*, in hand, when a horse is very clumsy, heavy in hand, stiff, headstrong, vicious, or apt to strike with his fore feet, or to rear or kick out behind, a stick, or pole, is very useful; the stick, (about seven feet long) is fastened by a strap and buckle through the eye of the snaffle, where the reins pass: a man places himself, at a certain distance, on the side of the horse's head,

head, going before him over the ground to be worked upon, and holds the ftick at arm's length, having tied it fo, as to leave it room to play, as he draws it gently backwards and forwards to refrefh and enliven the mouth. The other man holds a long rein, and the *chambriere*, as reprefented in *Plate* 7. Like the pillars, this leffon is excellent, or bad, according to the hands it is in. I have known a horfe's jaw broke, and his tongue cut in two by it, and therefore it muft be ufed in the moft fkilful and temperate manner, or not at all: it is ufeful in raifing horfe's heads; of thofe, particularly, who are apt to get their heads down, or to kick in piaffing on forwards, &c. Almoft any leffons may be done by the help of this pole.

To work in hand, the head and the croup, to the wall, *(Plate* 8.) two ftrings fixed, as above defcribed, (only that they muft not come at all through the large ring on the pad, but from the fmall rings on the head-ftall, immediately into the hand of the perfon who holds the *chambriere)* muft be ufed, one on each fide: one ftring, indeed, might do; the right one, in working to the right, and

fo

so *vice verſâ*: but two are much better, and often neceſ-ſary, to help to keep the horſe in a proper poſition. Paſ-ſing the ſtrings through the rings on the head-ſtall, is not neceſſary, when the horſe carries his fore-hand high, and well; and when they do paſs through them, great care muſt be taken, by a gentle uſe of them, that they do not gag the horſe: theſe two ſtrings muſt be buckled together, and meet in the hand of the perſon who holds the *cham-briere*, and who is on the left ſide of the horſe: the ſnaffle reins too muſt be joined, and the perſon near the horſe, who holds them, muſt alſo be on the left ſide of him, and near his ſhoulder, holding the right rein of the ſnaffle the ſhorteſt, to bend him that way, (as does alſo the right ſtring kept the tighteſt in the other perſon's hand) and making uſe alſo of the left rein, when neceſſary, to keep the horſe in a proper poſition, and to guide him occaſionally, as if he was upon him: and never ſo, as to take away from the bend. The leſſon of the head, or croupe, to the wall, in hand, is often done better, when the man who follows, and holds the *chambriere*, has no long reins, or only one long rein, unleſs the horſe is very aukward, refractory, or playful; for one of the long reins

reins is apt to get into the way of the man, who is nearer to the horse. When only one long rein is used, it will be, of course, the right hand one, to the right, and so *vice versâ*. And indeed, in other lessons in hand, these long reins are no longer necessary, when the horse is grown handy; provided the man nearer to him has a feeling, sensible, good hand, and perfectly knows what he is about. On the head or croup to the wall, in hand, it is a good way, at first, to have a man, holding a long string buckled simply to the eye of the snaffle, go before the horse, leading him; as it were, along the wall. Horses will, with care and patience, not be very long before they work well in hand; though, indeed, never so truly, or delicately, as under a good rider. Horses worked well in hand look particularly well in coming up the middle, and backing there on the piaffer, as also in the piaffer, in one place, both bent, *(Plate 9.)* and straight, animated properly, and kept in a good position, their mouths being properly played with, and humoured. When horses become free, and familiar with this method of working them in hand, it should be done by degrees on all paces, fast, and slow, but always without noife, hurry, or confufion. Nothing determines them better than working them in hand, when it is well done. As the want of great accuracy, and delicacy is, from the great numbers, in fome meafure unavoidable in military fchools, it is not amifs to teach troop horfes a little their leffons in hand, before the men do them on their backs. One of thefe ftrings may be ufed by the perfon who holds the *chambriere* on foot, when the horfe is mounted; and it is a good method to do fo, fometimes, on all leffons, and on all figures. This ftring faftened, as in the *epaule en dedans*, only that it goes immediately from the eye of the fnaffle into the hand of the perfon on foot, who muft ftand in the center of the circle, helps the perfon upon the horfe in the longe very much to bend him, as it does indeed in all other leffons. When the horfe has a rider on him, only one ftring is neceffary to be held by the perfon on foot. In the head to the wall, croup to the wall, piaffing, &c. &c. it muft be fhifted (for example, in the head to the wall, &c. &c. to the right) under the horfe's jaw, from through the right eye of the fnaffle, into the hand of the perfon on foot, who is on the left of the horfe; for it need not pafs through the fmall ring on the head-ftall

of

BREAKING HORSES, &c.

of the fnaffle; the man upon the horfe being the proper perfon to keep the horfe's head up. It is fometimes expedient to pafs the ftring over the horfe's neck under the rider's hand, inftead of under the horfe's jaw. It muft be fixed, in the firft place, like a running fnafflle, to the fkirts of the faddle, from whence it goes, as above-mentioned, through the eye of the fnaffle into the hand of the perfon on foot, after having paffed under the horfe's jaw. To piaffer too without any rider, on fquare, and all other figures, advancing gently, and well into the corners, is a very good leffon. One man muft ftand exactly before the horfe, with his face to him, holding the two eyes of the fnaffle, and keep the horfe advancing gently, by going backwards himfelf. The man with the *chambriere* muft ftand behind the horfe, and animate him, or not, as he finds neceffary. Backing the horfe fo too fometimes is ufeful: that may alfo be done on all figures. The degree of vivacity, or dulnefs in the horfe, muft determine how the man with the *chambriere* is to act, and where he is to place himfelf, when the horfe is backing. A horfe when well taught may be worked, and it is then the beft way, by a fingle man with long reins, and a *chambriere*, without any other perfon to affift. *(Plate* 10.) All airs in hand are to be worked fo, whenever the animal is become fupple and obedient.

Working in hand is very particularly ufeful in Military Equitation, becaufe it fpares the horfe the fatigue of any weight upon him; and the want of a proper allowance of corn, to enable horfes to go through the work with vigour, is a general army complaint, almoft in all European fervices. When it is well done, it has a mafterly, active appearance, and is always very ufeful in fuppling and determining horfes; but, paft all doubt, a good rider mounted, who feels every motion of the horfe, muft act with more precifion, delicacy, and exactnefs.

Great part of what has been faid here, of working in hand, belongs properly to other chapters, but I was unwilling to divide the fubject, and have therefore placed here what I had to mention about it.

CHAP.

C H A P. IV.

Of the head to the wall, and of the croup to the wall.

THIS leſſon ſhould be practiſed immediately after that of the *epaule en dedans,* in order to place the horſe properly the way he goes, &c. The difference between the head to the wall, and the croup to the wall, conſiſts in this: in the former, the fore-parts are more remote from the center, and go over more ground; in the latter, the hinder-parts are more remote from the center, and conſequently go over more ground: in both, as likewiſe in all other leſſons, (thoſe done in backing only excepted) the ſhoulders muſt go firſt. In riding-houſes, the head to the wall is the eaſier leſſon of the two, at firſt, the line to be worked upon being marked by the wall, which is not far from the horſe's head. All leſſons ought to be frequently varied, to prevent *routine.*

The motion of the legs in the leſſon we are ſpeaking of, to the right, is the ſame as that of the *epaule en dedans* to the left, and ſo *vice verſâ*; but the head is always bent and

and turned differently : in the *epaule en dedans*, the horse looks the contrary way to that which he goes ; in this he looks the way he is going.

In the beginning, very little bend must be required ; demanding too much at once would perplex the horse, and make him defend himself: it is to be augmented by degrees. If the horse absolutely refuses to obey, it is most probably a sign that either he or his rider has not been sufficiently prepared by previous lessons. It may happen, that weakness, or a hurt in some part of the body, or sometimes temper, though seldom, (in the horse I mean) may be the cause of the horse's defending himself: 'tis the rider's business to find out from whence the obstacle arises, and to remove it; and if he finds it to be from the first mentioned cause, the previous lessons must be resumed again for some time ; if from the second, proper remedies must be applied; and if from the last cause, when all fair means that can be tried, have failed, proper corrections, with coolness and judgment, must be used.

In practising this lesson to the right, bend the horse to the right with the right rein, helping the left leg over the
right,

right, (at the same time when the right leg is just come to the ground) with the left rein crossed towards the right, and keeping the right shoulder back with the right rein towards your body, in order to facilitate the left leg's crossing over the right ; and so *vice versâ* to the left, each rein helping the other by their properly-mixed effects. In working to the right, the rider's left leg helps the hinder parts on to the right, and his right leg stops them, if they get too much so ; and so *vice versâ* to the left ; but neither ought to be used, 'till the hand, being employed, (as has before been explained) in a proper manner, has failed, or finds, that a greater force is necessary to bring what is required about, than it can effect alone ; for the legs should not only be corresponding with the hand, but also subservient to it ; and all unnecessary aids, as well as all force, ought always to be avoided as much as possible. In first beginning to teach this lesson, the croup must be but little constrained ; as the horse grows more supple, engage it more by degrees.

In the execution of all lessons, the equilibre of the rider's body is of great use, ease and help to the horse : it ought

ought always to go with and accompany every motion of the animal; when to the right, to the right; and when to the left, to the left; if it does not, it is a very great hinderance to the horse's going.

This lesson is perpetually of service; for example, in all openings and closings of files: and though it be chiefly employed on straight lines, neverthelefs it must be practised, advancing, retreating, turning, &c. as it may be of essential use almost in all cases whatever: it must be practised too in all paces, very fast as well as very slow, but of course gently at first; and changes also from one hand to the other must frequently be made on two pistes. 'Tis natural to imagine, that some horses, as well as some men, will be found more or less intelligent, active, vigorous, and supple, than others; and accordingly more or less is to be demanded and expected from them. This and all other lessons are to be performed with or without a longe, as may be found needful.

Upon all horses, in every lesson and action, it must be observed, that there is no horse but has his own peculiar *appui* or degree of bearing, and also a sensibility of mouth,

BREAKING HORSES, &c.

as likewife a rate of his own, which it is abfolutely neceffary for the rider to difcover and make himfelf acquainted
with. A bad rider always takes off at leaft the delicacy of
both, if not abfolutely deftroys it, which is generally the
cafe. The horfe will inform his rider when he has got his
proper bearing in the mouth, by playing pleafantly and
fteadily with his bit, and by the fpray about his chaps. A
delicate and good hand will not only always preferve
a light *appui*, or bearing in its fenfibility, but alfo of a
heavy one, whether naturally fo or acquired, make a light
one. The lighter this *appui* can be made, the better;
but the rider's hand muft correfpond with it: if it does
not, the more the horfe is properly prepared, fo much the
worfe for the rider. Inftances of this inconvenience of the
beft of *appui*'s, when the rider is not equally taught with
the horfe, may be feen every day in fome gentlemen, who
try to get their horfes bitted, as they call it, (which now
and then, though very rarely, they get done to fome degree) without being fuitably prepared themfelves for riding them: the confequence of which is, that they ride
in danger of breaking their necks: 'till at length, after
much hauling about, and by the joint infenfibility and ignorance

norance of themselves and their grooms, the poor animals gradually become mere senseless, unfeeling posts, and thereby grow, what they call, settled, and pleasant; that is to say, in reality, that they are grown as insensible as their riders, who, because they are void of feeling, and are not firm, must either hold by the bridle, or fall. One perpetually hears people say, they love a horse, who will let them bear a little on his mouth. Depend upon it, those people are not only ignorant, and unfeeling, but also very unfirm in their seat; for if they were not, they could not possibly find either use, or ease, in bearing a dead weight on their horses mouths. To help a horse every now and then, properly, is a very different, and a very useful thing. When the proper *appui* is found, and made of course as light as possible, it must not be kept dully fixed without any variation, but be played with; otherwise one equally continued tension of reins, though not a violent one, would render both the rider's hand, and the horse's mouth very dull. The slightest, and frequent giving, and taking is therefore necessary to keep both perfect.

Whatever pace or degree of quickness you work in, (be it ever so fast, or ever so slow) it must be cadenced; time is as necessary for an horseman, as for a musician.

Every soldier must be very well instructed in this lesson of the head and of the tail to the wall: scarce any manœuvre can be well performed without it. In closing and opening of files, it is almost every moment wanted. Few regimental riding-masters either practise it right, teach it right, or know it right, but act by force only: and make the horse look the wrong way. It is a great detriment to the service, that so few of the teachers are instructed on true and useful principles of horsemanship. This lesson of the head, or croup to the wall, &c. and all others, may be done on any pace; but, for the reasons given at the end of the sixth chapter, I shall give no very full instructions for them on a gallop here, as the nature of army riding hardly permits soldiers to be taught so far with exactness. If a horse is well taught on ever so slow a pace, he may, by degrees, without difficulty, be taught to do the same lesson with any degree of velocity. When he does it on a gallop, the rider must be quiet, and exact in the changes, and be then careful to ſtop the horſe's leg, with which he leads, juſt at the time when it is moſt forward, before it comes to the ground, by means of a ſlight tenſion of the rein on the ſame ſide, which will of courſe make the other leg go forward, and lead ; and, that the horſe may change his hinder leg at the ſame time, which is abſolutely neceſſary, the rider muſt at the ſame time croſs over his hand, (to the left, for example, in changing from the left to the right) replacing it properly the moment the horſe has changed both before and behind, which muſt be done at the ſame time.

CHAP.

CHAP. V.

The Trot.

THE three different kinds of trot, the extended, the supple, and the even, or equal, *(le determiné le deli?, & l'uni)* are explained so wonderfully masterly, and elegantly, in Monsieur BOURGELAT's *Nouveau Newcastle,* that I can not omit giving here the chapter on trots of so truly admirable a master, for which I am obliged to Mr. BERENGER's translation of that excellent work.

" When a horse trots, his legs are in this position, two in the air, and two upon the ground, at the same time crosswise; that is to say, the near foot before, and the off foot behind are off the ground, and the other two upon it, and so alternately of the other two. This action of his legs is the same as when he walks, except that in the trot his motions are more quick. All writers, both ancient and modern, have constantly asserted the trot to be the foundation of every lesson you can teach a horse : there are none, likewife, who have not thought proper to give general rules upon this fubject, but none have been exact enough to defcend into a detail of particular rules, and to diftinguifh fuch cafes as are different, and admit of exceptions, though fuch often are found from the different make and tempers of horfes, as they happen to be more or lefs fuited to what they are deftined; fo that, by following their general maxims, many horfes have been fpoiled, and made heavy and aukward, inftead of becoming fupple and active, and as much mifchief has been occafioned by adopting their principles, although juft, as if they had been fuggefted by ignorance itfelf. Three qualities are effentially neceffary to make the trot ufeful. It ought to be extended, fupple, and even, or equal. Thefe three qualities are related to, and mutually depend upon each other; in effect, you cannot pafs to the fupple trot, without having firft worked upon the extended trot; and you can never arrive at the even and equal trot, without having firft practifed the fupple. I mean by the extended, that trot, in which the horfe trots out without retaining himfelf, being quite ftrait, and going directly forwards; this confequently is the kind of trot with which you muft

begin;

begin; for before any thing else should be thought of, the horse should be taught to embrace, and cover his ground readily, and without fear. The trot however may be extended without being supple, for the horse may go directly forward, and yet not have that ease, and suppleness of limb, which distinguishes, and characterises the supple. I define the supple trot to be that, in which the horse at every motion that he makes, bends and plays all his joints, that is to say, those of his shoulders, his knees, and feet, which no colts or raw horses can execute, who have not had their limbs suppled by exercise, and who generally trot with a surprizing stiffness, and aukwardness, without the least spring or play in their joints. The even or equal trot, is that wherein the horse makes all his limbs and joints move so equally, and exactly, that his legs never cover more ground one than the other, nor at one time more than another. To do this, the horse must of necessity unite and collect all his strength, and, if I may be allowed the expression, distribute it equally through all his joints. To go from the extended trot to the supple, you must gently, and by degrees hold in your horse, and when by exercise he has attained sufficient ease and suppleness to manage his limbs readily, you muſt infenſibly hold him in ſtill more and more, and by degrees you will lead him to the equal trot. The trot is the firſt exerciſe to which a horſe is put; this is a neceſſary leſſon, but, if given unſkilfully, it loſes its end, and even does harm. Horſes of a hot, and fretful temper, have generally too great a diſpoſition to the extended trot; never abandon theſe horſes to their will, hold them in, pacify them, moderate their motions by retaining them judiciouſly; their limbs will grow ſupple, and they will acquire at the ſame time that union and equality which is ſo eſſentially neceſſary. If you have a horſe that is heavy, conſider if this heavineſs, or ſtiffneſs of his ſhoulders, or legs, is owing to a want of ſtrength, or of ſuppleneſs; whether it proceeds from his having been exerciſed unſkilfully, too much, or too little. If he is heavy, becauſe the motions of his legs and ſhoulders are naturally cold, and ſluggiſh, though at the ſame time his limbs are good, and his ſtrength is only confined, and ſhut up, if I may ſo ſay, a moderate, but continual exerciſe of the trot will open and ſupple his joints, and render the action of his ſhoulders and legs more free, and bold; hold him in the hand, and ſupport him

BREAKING HORSES, &c.

in his trot, but take care to do it so as not to check, or slacken his pace; aid him, and drive him forward while you support him; remember at the same time, that if he is loaded with a great head, the continuation of the trot will make his *appui* hard and dull, because he will by this means abandon himself still more, and weigh upon the hand. All horses that are inclined to be *ramingue*, that is to say, to retain themselves, and to resist by so doing, should be kept to the extended trot. Every horse, who has a tendency to be *ramingue*, is naturally disposed to unite himself, and collect all his strength; your only way with such horses is to force them forward; in the instant that he obeys, and goes freely on, retain him a little, yield your hand immediately after, and you will find soon that the horse of himself will bend his joints, and go united and equally. A horse of a sluggish and cold disposition, which has nevertheless strength and bottom, should likewise be put to the extended trot. As he grows animated, and begins to go free, keep him together by little and little, in order to lead him insensibly to the supple trot: but if while you keep him together, you perceive that he slackens his action, and retains himself, give him the aids briskly, and push him forward, keeping him neverthelefs gently in hand; by this means he will be taught to trot freely, and equally at the fame time. If a horfe of a cold, and fluggifh temper, is weak in his legs, and reins, you muft manage him cautioufly in working him in the trot, otherwife you will enervate, and fpoil him. Befides, in order to make the moft of a horfe who is not ftrong, endeavour to give him wind, by working him flowly, and at intervals, and by encreafing the vigour of his exercife by degrees; for you muft remember, that you ought always to difmifs your horfe before he is fpent, and overcome by fatigue; never pufh your leffons too far, in hopes of fuppling your horfe's limbs by the trot, inftead of this you will falfify, and harden his *appui*, which is a cafe that happens but too frequently. Farther, it is of importance to remark, that you ought at no time, neither in the extended, fupple, or equal trot, to confine your horfe in the hand, in expectation of raifing him, and fixing his head in a proper place. If his *appui* be full in hand, and the action of his trot fhould be checked, and reftrained by the power of the bridle, his bars would very foon grow callous, and his mouth be hardened, and

BREAKING HORSES, &c.

and dead; if, on the contrary, he has a fine, and senfible mouth, this very reftraint would offend, and make him uneafy; you muft endeavour then, as has already been faid, to give him by degrees, and infenfibly, the true and juft *appui*, to place his head, and form his mouth by ftops, and half-ftops, by fometimes moderating and reftraining him, with a gentle, and light hand, and yielding it to him immediately again, and by fometimes letting him trot without feeling the bridle at all. There is a difference between horfes who are heavy in the hand, and fuch as endeavour to force it: the firft fort lean, and throw all their weight upon the hand, either as they happen to be weak, or too heavy, and clumfy in their foreparts, or from having their mouths too flefhy and grofs, and confequently dull and infenfible: the fecond pull againft the hand, becaufe their bars are hard, lean, and generally round: the firft may be brought to go equal, and upon their haunches, by means of the trot, and flow gallop; and the other may be made light and active by art, and by fettling them well in their trot, which will alfo give them ftrength and vigour. Horfes of the firft fort are generally fluggifh; the other kind are, for the moft part, impatient, and difobedient, and upon that very account more dangerous, and incorrigible. The only proof, or rather the moſt certain ſign of your horſe's trotting well, is, that when he is in his trot, and you begin to preſs him a little, he offers to gallop. After having trotted your horſe ſufficiently upon a ſtrait line, or directly forwards, work him upon circles, but before you put him to this, walk him gently round the circle, that he may apprehend and know the ground he is to go over. This being done, work him in the trot. A horſe that is loaded before, and heavily made, will find more pains and difficulty in uniting his ſtrength, in order to be able to turn, than in going ſtrait forward. The action of turning tries the ſtrength of his reins, and employs his memory and attention; therefore let one part of your leſſons be to trot them ſtrait forward: finiſh them in the ſame manner, obſerving that the intervals between the ſtops (which you ſhould make very often) be long, or ſhort, as you judge neceſſary. I ſay, you ſhould make frequent ſtops, for they often ſerve as a correction to horſes that abandon themſelves, force the hand, or bear too much upon it in their trot. There are ſome horſes who are ſupple in

their

BREAKING HORSES, &c.

their shoulders, but who neverthelefs abandon themfelves, this fault is occafioned by the rider's having often held his bridle hand too tight in working them upon large circles; to remedy this, trot them upon one line or tread, and very large; ftop them often, keeping back your body and outward leg, in order to make them bend and play their haunches. The principal effects then of the trot are to make a horfe light, and active, and to give him a juft *appui*. In reality, in this action he is always fupported on one fide by one of his fore legs, and on the other by one of his hind legs: now the fore and hind parts being equally fupported crofswife, the rider cannot fail of fuppling, and loofening his limbs, and fixing his head; but if the trot difpofes, and prepares the fpirits and motions of a finewy and active horfe for the jufteft leffons, if it calls out and unfolds the powers, and ftrength of the animal, which before were buried, and fhut up, if I may ufe the expreffion, in the ftiffnefs of his joints and limbs; if this firft exercife, to which you put your horfe, is the foundation of all the different airs, and maneges, it ought to be given in proportion to the ftrength and vigour of the horfe. To judge of this, you muft go farther than mere outward appearances. A horse may be but weak in the reins, and yet execute some air, and accompany it with vigour, as long as his strength is united and entire; but if he becomes disunited, by having been worked beyond his ability in the trot, he will then faulter in his air, and perform it without vigour or grace. There are also some horses who are very strong in the loins, but who are weak in their limbs; these are apt to retain themselves, they bend, and sink in their trot, and go as if they were afraid of hurting their shoulders, their legs or feet. This irresolution proceeds only from a natural sense they have of their weakness. This kind of horses should not be too much exercised in the trot, nor have sharp correction; their shoulders, legs, or hocks, would be weakened and injured; so that learning in a little time to hang back, and abandon themselves on the *appui*, they would never be able to furnish any air with vigour, and justness. Let every lesson then be well weighed; the only method by which success can be insured, is the discretion you shall use in giving them in proportion to the strength of the horse, and from your sagacity in deciding upon what air or manege is most proper for him, to which you must be directed by observing which seems most suited to his inclination and capacity.

CHAP.

CHAP. VI.

The method of reining back---and of moving forwards immediately after---of piaffing---of pillars, &c.---of moving pillars, &c.

SOMETHING having already been said, in the chapter of suppling, &c. upon the subject of reining back, there will not be occasion to dwell much upon it here, as the reader may have recourse to that chapter. Horses, particularly such as are never put in the pillars, nor taught to piaffe, should be reined back a good deal, sometimes slow, sometimes fast, and always without confusion, both in hand, and when rode. Never finish your work by reining back, especially with horses that have any disposition towards retaining themselves; but always move them forwards, and a little upon the haunches also after it, before you dismount; unless they retain themselves very much indeed, in which case nothing at all must be demanded from the haunches, but, quite the contrary, they must immediately be trotted hard out. This lesson of reining back, and piaffing, is excellent to conclude with, and puts a horse well and properly on the haunches: the head and fore-parts must be kept high, and free, for any confinement there destroys action. To bend the horses sometimes in doing it, is a good lesson. It may be done, according as horses are more or less suppled, either going forwards, backing, or in the same place: if 'tis done well advancing, or at most, on the same spot, it is full sufficient for a soldier's horse: for to piaffe in backing, is rather too much to be expected in the hurry, which cannot but attend such numbers both of men and horses, as must be taught together in regiments. This lesson must never be attempted at all, 'till horses are very well suppled, and somewhat accustomed to be put together; otherwise it will have very bad consequences, and create restiveness: infallibly so, if not practised with the utmost exactness and delicacy; and principally with horses, that have the least tendency to retain, or to defend themselves. If they refuse to back, and stand motionless, the rider's legs must be approached with the greatest gentleness to the horse's sides; at the same time as the hand is acting on the reins to solicit the horse's backing. This seldom fails of procuring

curing the defired effect, by raifing one of the horfe's fore legs, which being in the air, has no weight upon it, and is confequently very eafily brought backwards by a fmall degree of tenfion in the reins. When this leffon of piaffing is well performed, it is very noble, and ufeful, and has a pleafing air; it is an excellent one to begin teaching fcholars with. In regiments, at their firft being raifed, when all horfes are brought in young and raw, there can of courfe be no horfes ready prepared in it for this purpofe; but a litle time and diligence remedies this inconvenience.

The leffon, we are fpeaking of, is particularly ferviceable in the pillars, for placing fcholars well at firft. Very few regimental riding-houfes have pillars, and I muft fay, that it is fortunate they have not; for though, when properly made ufe of with fkill, they are one of the greateft and beft difcoveries in horfemanfhip, they muft be allowed to be very dangerous and pernicious, when they are not under the direction of a very knowing perfon. Upon the whole, however highly I approve of pillars, I would on no account admit of any, unlefs conftantly under the eye and attention of a very intelligent teacher; which is a thing

L

so difficult to be found in regiments, that I think pillars are better banished from amongst them, and therefore shall say no more here of what I esteem neverthelefs so much. As for the single pillar, used in the manner it formerly was, it is a very useless and ridiculous thing; and being, as I hope and believe, universally laid aside, I think it not worth making further mention of here. Moving pillars are exempt from those inconveniences which attend fixed ones, and I therefore recommend them for army riding. By moving pillars, I understand a horse held by a rein on each side, by a man on each side of him: another person with a *chambriere* follows, animates, or sooths him, as he finds necessary, and makes him piaffe backwards, or forwards, with, or without long reins, as is found expedient. When the long reins, or strings are used, or rather the long string or rein, (for one is generally sufficient) it must be fixed on the side the horse is to be bent: this string is fixed to the saddle, and goes through the eye of the snaffle, and also through a ring on the head-stall, if the horse is apt to get his head low: one man, besides the one who holds the *chambriere*, is sufficient in this case: the horse is bent to the right, or left, or kept wholly strait. This method

thod is particularly useful for horses whose action of their hinder legs is confined, and wants liberty: the same rule will hold good for all horses so circumstanced in all they do; for they should always be worked boldly out on large scales, and never confined to small figures. A horse looks remarkably well in this attitude, if those who hold him have light hands, and keep his head high: they should each of them have a switch, to help them to keep the horse straight, in case of necessity. This lesson may be very well done by one man alone, with long reins *(as in Plate* 10.)

It would scarce be possible (neither is it indeed necessary) to teach the more refined and difficult parts of horsemanship to all the different kinds, and dispositions, both of men and horses, which are in all regiments; or to find the time and attention requisite for it to such numbers; but I yet hope some proper institution will be formed, to make good riding-masters, farriers, sadlers, and gun-smiths, and every thing else necessary for the army, upon a good, and proper footing: they are absolutely necessary, and should be properly and equally divided through the regiment, in the squadrons and troops. There should be one riding-master in chief, with a fufficient number of under ones under him, and formed by him: he fhould infpect the work of the others very frequently, and give leffons by turns to the whole regiment, going about from one quarter to another, if the regiment is feparated: he fhould break too the officers horfes, or rather teach them to do it themfelves, who, I am forry to fay it, ftand at prefent, in general, in the greateft need of inftructions,---no people more: they fhould, therefore, and for the fake of creating emulation too in the men by their example, always attend the riding-mafter regularly two or three times a week, at leaft. I muft urge the neceffity of forming by reading, and ferious ftudy, as well as by much conftant practice, proper riding-mafters for the army; though I am thoroughly apprized, as the celebrated Mr. BOURGELAT obferves, that an ill-founded prejudice partially directs the judgment of the greater part of thofe people, who call themfelves conoiffeurs. I know full well that they fuppofe that practice alone can infure perfection, and that in their arguments in favour of this their deplorable fyftem, they reject with fcorn all books, and authors: but Equitation is confeffedly a fcience; every fcience is founded upon principles, and theory muft must indispensably be necessary, because what is truly just and beautiful can not depend upon chance. What indeed is to be expected from a man, who has no other guide than a long continued practice, and who must of necessity labour under very great uncertainties! Incapable of accounting rationally for what he does, it must be impossible for him to enlighten me, or communicate to me the knowledge which he fancies himself possessed of. How then can I look upon such a man as a master? On the other hand, what advantages may I not obtain from the instructions of a person, whom theory enables to comprehend and feel the effects of his slightest operations, and who can explain to me such principles, as an age of constant practice only could never put me into a way of acquiring? Equitation does, to be sure, require also a constant, and an assiduous exercise. Habit, and continual practice will go a great way in all exercises, which depend on the mechanism of the body, but, unless this mechanism is properly fixed, and supported on the solid basis of theory, errors will be the inevitable consequence. In working a horse, a principal object should be to exercise the genius, and memory of the animal, as well as his body. You should

should endeavour to discover his natural inclination, and to get a thorough knowledge of his abilities, in order to take advantage in future of that knowledge. Without the help of lights derived from just principles, it is morally impossible that a horseman should make use of his reason upon all occasions, or be able to find out, with care and attention, whatever may conduct him to the end and object of his hopes, desires, and undertakings; because, in few words, there is an absolute necessity of some method for improving the natural disposition of the animal, which is in some cases defective and intractable. The consequences of the false, and prejudicial system, which I am opposing, justify my assertions. The knowledge of a horse is vulgarly thought so familiar, and the means of dressing him so general, and so common, that you can hardly meet with a man, who does not flatter himself, that he has succeeded in both points; and while masters, who sacrifice every hour of their life to attain knowledge, still find themselves immerged in darkness and obscurity, men the most uninformed imagine, that they have attained the summit of perfection, and in consequence thereof suppress the least inclination of learning even the first elements.

A

A blind, and boundlefs prefumption is the characteriftic of ignorance; the fruits of long ftudy, and application amount to a difcovery of innumerable frefh difficulties, at the fight of which a diligent man, very far from over-rating his own merit, redoubles his efforts in purfuit of further knowledge.

CHAP.

C H A P. VII.

The method of teaching horses to stand fire, noises, alarms, fights, &c.---of preventing their lying down in the water--to stand quiet to be shot off from---to go over rough and bad ground ---to leap hedges, gates, ditches, &c. standing and flying---to disregard dead horses---to swim, &c.

IN order to make horses stand fire, the sound of drums, and all sorts of different noises, you must use them to it by degrees in the stable at feeding-time; and instead of being frightened at it, they will soon come to like it, as a signal for eating.

With regard to such horses as are afraid of burning objects, begin by keeping them still at a certain distance from some lighted straw: caress the horse, and in proportion as his fright diminishes, approach gradually the burning straw very gently, and increase the size of it. By this means he will very quickly be brought to be so familiar with it, as to walk undaunted even through it. The same

BREAKING HORSES, &c.

same method and gentleness must be observed also, in regard to glittering arms, colours, standards, &c.

As to horses that are apt to lie down in the water, if animating them, and attacking them vigorously, should fail of the desired effect, (which seldom is the case) then break a straw-bottle full of water upon their heads, the moment they begin to lie down, and let the water run into their ears, which is a thing they apprehend very much, and which will in all probability soon cure them of the trick.

All troop-horses must be taught to stand quiet and still when they are shot off from, to stop the moment you present, and not to move after firing, 'till they are required to do it: this lesson ought especially to be observed in light troops, and it should never be neglected in any kind of cavalry whatsoever: in short, the horses must be taught to be so cool and undisturbed, as to suffer the riders to act upon them with the same freedom, as if they were on foot. Patience, coolness, and temper, are the only means requisite for accomplishing this end.

A METHOD OF

The rider, when he fires, must be very attentive not to throw himself forwards too much, or otherwise *derange* himself in his seat. Begin by walking the horse gently, then stop and keep him from stirring for some time, so as to accustom him by degrees not to have the least idea of moving without orders: if he does, back him; and when you stop him, and he is quite still, leave the reins quite loose, and caress him.

To use a horse to fire-arms, first put a pistol or carbine in the manger with his feed; then use him to the sound of the lock and the pan; after which, when you are upon him, shew the piece to him, presenting it forwards, sometimes on one side, sometimes on the other: when he is thus far reconciled, proceed to flash in the pan; after which, put a small charge into the piece, and so continue augmenting it by degrees to the quantity which is commonly used: if he seems uneasy, walk him forwards a few steps slowly, and then stop, back, move forwards, then stop again, and caress him. Great care must be taken not to burn, or singe the horse any where in firing; he would remember it, and be very shy, for a long time. Horses are

are also often disquieted and unsteady at the clash and glittering of arms, at the drawing and returning of swords, all which they must be familiarized to by little and little, by frequency and gentleness.

In going over rough and bad ground, the men must keep their hands high, and their bodies back.

It is very expedient for all cavalry, in general, but particularly for light cavalry, that their horses should be very ready and expert in leaping over ditches, hedges, gates, &c. not only singly but in squadrons, and lines. The leaps, of whatever sort they are, which the horses are brought to in the beginning, ought to be very small ones, and as the horse improves in his leaping, be augmented by degrees; for if the leaps were encreased considerably at once, the horse would blunder, grow fearful, and contract an aukward way of leaping with hurry, and confusion. The riders must keep their bodies back, raise their hand a little in order to help the fore-parts of the horse up, and be very attentive to their equilibre, without raising themselves up in the saddle, or moving their arms. The surest way to prevent people, in leaping over any thing, from raising up their arms and elbows, (which is an unfirm, and ungraceful motion) is to make them put a hand whip, or switch, under each arm, and not let them drop. 'Tis best to begin at a low bar covered with furze, *(Plate* 15 .3.) which pricking the horse's legs, if he does not raise himself sufficiently, prevents his contracting a sluggish and dangerous habit of touching, as he goes over, which any thing yielding, and not pricking, would give him a custom of doing. Many horses, in learning to leap, are apt to come too near, and in a manner with their feet under the bar. The best way to prevent their doing so, is to place under the bar two planks of the breadth of the pillars on which the leaping bar is fixed: these planks must meet and join at top under the bar, about two feet high from the ground, *(Plate* 15 .4.) and project at bottom upon the ground, about two feet; they must be strongly framed, that the horse may not break them, by touching them with his feet. The bar should be placed so as to run round, when touched. Let the ditches and hedges, &c. you first bring horses to, be inconsiderable, and in this, as in every thing else, let the increase be made by degrees. Accustom them to come up gently to every thing, which they are

BREAKING HORSES, &c.

are to leap over, and to stand coolly at it for some time; and then to raise themselves gently up, and go clear over it, without either sloth or hurry. When they leap well standing, *(Plate* 11 *and* 13.) then use them to walk gently up to the leap, and to go over it without first halting at it; and after that practice is familiar to them, repeat the like in a gentle trot, and so by degrees faster and faster, 'till at length it is as familiar to them to leap flying on a full gallop, *(Plate* 12 *and* 14.) as any other way; all which is to be acquired with great facility by calm and soft means, without any hurry.

As horses are naturally apt to be frightened at the sight and smell of dead horses, numbers of which are every moment met with on service, (especially at the latter end of the year, when the roads are bad, and the poor animals, too often treated and driven cruelly, go a great way from camp for forage) it is adviseable to habituate them to walk over, and leap over carcases of dead horses; and as they are particularly terrified at this sight, the greater gentleness ought consequently to be used in breaking them of their dread of it.

Horses

Horses should also be accustomed to swim, which often may be necessary upon service; and if the men and horses both are not used to it, both may be frequently liable to perish in the water. A very small portion of strength is sufficient to guide a horse, any where indeed, but partiticularly in the water, where they must be permitted to have their heads, and be as little constrained as possible in any shape. In crossing rivers, the horse's head should be kept against the current, more or less, according to the situation of the place, higher up, or lower down, purposed to land at, and the degree of rapidity of the water. In going down the stream, the straighter the horse is the better. The rider had always better quit his stirrups on these occasions, for fear of accidents, and his getting entangled in them. A horse is turned difficultly in the water; it must be done very gently and carefully. For partizans, and all who go chiefly on reconnoitring duty, horses should be chosen, who are not apt to neigh: the Numidians preferred mares to horses, for surprizes on the enemy, because, being less apt to neigh, they were less likely to be discovered. Those of the whole army should be taught to be obedient to the voice, and to carry double.

BREAKING HORSES, &c.

ble. Reins may be cut in battle; and in croſſing waters, and upon forced marches, it may ſometimes be neceſſary to take the infantry *(en croupe)* up behind. The ancient Lybians directed their horſes in battle by the voice; and the ſame cuſtom prevails amongſt them to this day, for the modern Africans do the ſame.

The heavy cavalry may poſſibly object to having their large horſes taught all theſe ſeveral exerciſes; but though they are not, nor can indeed be expected to perform all; with the ſame activity and velocity, as light troops do, yet 'tis abſolutely neceſſary, that they ſhould be taught them all; for 'tis a melancholy conſideration, that any trifling obſtacle ſhould prevent ſo uſeful and powerful a body from acting. I cannot take upon me to ſay, whether it was always ſo in former times, or not: the ancients, I believe, underſtood horſemanſhip more than we are aware of: there is a great deal of good ſenſe in XENOPHON's method of forming horſes for war; after him, horſemanſhip was buried for ages, or rather brutaliſed, which is ſtill too much the caſe.

CHAP.

C H A P. VIII.

The method of curing reſtiveneſſes, vices, defences, ſtarting, and ſtumbling, &c.

BEFORE any mention is made of the different kinds of reſtiveneſſes, vices, and defences, &c. it is not amiſs to obſerve, that a horſe's being good or ill-natured greatly depends on the temper of the perſon, that is put about him, eſpecially at firſt; and conſequently one cannot be too careful and watchful in this point.

Whenever a horſe makes reſiſtance, one ought, before a remedy or correction is thought of, to examine very minutely all the tackle about him, if any thing hurts or tickles him, whether he has any natural or accidental weakneſs, or in ſhort any the leaſt impediment in any part. For want of this precaution, and previous inſpection, many fatal, and often irreparable diſaſters happen: the poor dumb animal is frequently accuſed falſely of being reſtive and vicious; is uſed ill without reaſon, and being forced into

deſpair,

BREAKING HORSES, &c.

despair, is, in a manner, obliged to act accordingly, be his temper and inclination ever so well disposed. It must never be forgot, that it is necessary to work on the minds of horses, at first by slow motions which give them time to reflect. By degrees every thing may be done most rapidly with ease and very well. Such is in general, unless spoilt by us, the good temper, docility, and obedience of a horse, that almost any thing may be done with him by good-nature, and science. Even the domestic, worthy, friendly dog is not more susceptible of education.

A horse that is vicious and also so weak, that there are no hopes of his growing stronger, is a most deplorable beast, and not worth any one's care or trouble: 'tis very seldom, (I was near saying, never) the case, that a horse is really, and by nature vicious; but if such be found, chastisements will become necessary sometimes, but they must then be always made use of with the greatest judgment, and temper. The propriety of aids is to foresee, and prevent faults. The propriety of chastisements is to correct them.

Correction, according as you use it, throws a horse into more or less violent action, which, if he be weak, he cannot support: but a vicious strong horse is to be considered in a very different light, being able both to undergo and consequently to profit by all lessons; and is, in every respect, far preferable to the best-natured weak one upon earth. Patience and science are never-failing means to reclaim a wicked horse: in whatsoever manner he defends himself, bring him back frequently with gentleness, but with firmness too, to the lesson which he seems most averse to. Horses are by degrees made obedient through the hope of recompence and the fear of punishment: how to mix these two motives judiciously together is a very difficult matter, not easy to be prescribed; it requires much thought and practice; and not only a good head, but a good heart likewise. The coolest, and best-natured rider, *cæteris paribus*, will always succeed best. By a dextrous use of the incitements above-mentioned you will gradually bring the horse to temper and obedience; mere force and want of skill and of coolness would only tend to confirm him in bad tricks. If he be impatient or choleric, never strike him, unless he absolutely refuses to go forwards,

which

BREAKING HORSES, &c.

which you muft refolutely oblige him to do, and which will be of itfelf a correction, by preventing his having time to meditate, and put in execution any defence by retaining himfelf. Refiftance in horfes, you muft confider, is fometimes a mark of ftrength and vigour, and proceeds from fpirits, as well as fometimes from vice and weaknefs. Weaknefs frequently drives horfes into vicioufnefs, when any thing, wherein ftrength is neceffary, is demanded from them; nay, it inevitably muft: great care therefore fhould always be taken to diftinguifh from which of thefe two caufes, that are evidently fo different, the defence arifes, before any remedy or punifhment is thought of. It may fometimes be a bad fign, when horfes do not at all defend themfelves, and proceed from a fluggifh difpofition, a want of fpirit, and of a proper fenfibility. Whenever one is fo fortunate as to meet with a horfe of juft the right fpirit, activity, delicacy of feeling, with ftrength, and good-nature, he cannot be cherifhed too much; for fuch a one is a rare and ineftimable jewel, and if properly treated, will, in a manner, do every thing of himfelf. Horfes are oftener fpoilt by having too much done to them, and by attempts to drefs them in too great a hurry, than by any other treatment.

If after a horse has been well suppled, and there are no impediments, either natural or accidental, if he still persists to defend himself, chastisements then become necessary: but whenever this is the case, they must not be frequent, but always firm, though always as little violent, as possible: for they are both dangerous and very prejudicial, when frequently or slightly played with; and still more so, when used too violently. When a rider quarrels with his horse, he is generally the dupe of his passion, and the fray commonly ends to his disadvantage. Whenever you see a man beating any animal, you will almost always find, that the man is in the wrong, and the animal in the right.

'Tis impossible in general, to be too circumspect in lessons of all kinds, in aids, chastisements or caresses; for as the great Duke of Newcastle observes, if any man was in the form of a horse, he could not invent with more art than some horses do, schemes to oppose what is required of him. Some have quicker parts, and more cunning, than others. Many will imperceptibly gain a little every day on their rider. Various in short are their dispositions, and capacities. It is the rider's business to find out their **different qualities,**
and

and to make them sensible how much he loves them, and desires to be loved by them, but at the same time, that he does not fear them, and will be master. A good natured clever man may with the greatest ease teach a horse any thing; more tricks even of all kinds, than dogs are seen to perform at fairs. Plunging is a very common defence among restive and vicious horses: if they do it in the same place or backing, they must by the rider's legs, and spurs too sometimes firmly applied, be obliged to go forwards, and their heads kept up high. But if they do it flying forwards, keep them back, ride them gently and very slow for a good while together, and back them gently every now and then. Of all bad tempers and qualities in horses, those, which are occasioned by harsh treatment and ignorant riders, which are very common, are the worst.

Rearing is a bad vice, and in weak horses especially, a very dangerous one. Whilst the horse is up, the rider must yield his hand, and when the horse is descending he must vigorously determine him forwards by approaching his legs to the horse's sides: if this be done at any other time, but whilst the horse is coming down, it may add a spring to his

rearing,

rearing and make him fall backwards. With a good hand on them, horses seldom persist in this vice; for they are themselves naturally much afraid of falling backwards. If this method, which I have mentioned, fails, (which it scarcely ever will) you must make the horse kick up behind, by getting somebody on foot to strike him behind with a whip; or, if that will not effect it, by pricking him with a goad.

Starting often proceeds from a defect in the sight, which therefore must be carefully looked into. Whatever the horse is afraid of, bring him up to it gently; if you caress him every step he advances, he will go quite up to it by degrees, and soon grow familiar with all sorts of objects. Nothing but great gentleness can correct this fault: for if you inflict punishment, the apprehension of chastisement becomes prevalent, and causes more starting, than the fear of the object. If you let him go by the object, without bringing him up to it, you increase the fault and confirm him in his fear: the consequence of which is, he takes his rider perhaps a quite contrary way from what he was going, becomes his master, and puts himself and the person upon him, every moment in great danger. I have so often heard people maintain, some, that blows are necessary to cure
this

this evil; and others, that horses should be suffered to have their own way in it, that I could not help saying a few words upon this subject, (though it speaks for itself) to convince those, who, as my ingenious friend Mr. BOURGELAT says, *argumentent de ces systemes deplorables.*

Quarrelling with horses, plaguing, or beating them, as one often sees done, not only spoils both their tempers, and their paces, but it teaches them to trip, stumble, fall, start, run away, and to be unsteady and vicious, &c. whilst gentleness and coolness would very soon bring them to go through, or over any bad place whatsoever, with ease, good-humour and safety. Beat a horse for a trip, or such a kind of thing, and he will soon do it again through fear and hurry. Such failures sometimes proceed from weakness. In that case, proper food, and gentle exercise, by restoring the animal to health, and vigour, will cure him of them. If they come from inattention, or from the badness of his paces, he must have a good rider to render him attentive, and mend his movements. All other remedies will prove fruitless, but these will not, unless some natural defects, or acquired hurts, such as lameness, or bad weakening distempers interfere. Many

Many troop horses, and particularly old ones, often do not chuse to leave their companions. They should therefore be used early, and frequently to leave their ranks singly.

With such horses, as are to a very great degree fearful of any objects, make a quiet horse, by going before them, gradually entice them to approach nearer and nearer to the thing they are afraid of. If the horse, thus alarmed, be undisciplined and headstrong, he will probably run away with his rider; and if so, his head must be kept up high, and the snaffle sawed backwards and forwards from right to left, taking up and yielding the reins of it, as also the reins of the bit: but this latter must not be sawed backwards and forwards, like the snaffle, but only taken up, and yielded properly. No man ever yet did, or ever will stop a horse, or gain any one point over him by main force, or violence, or by pulling a dead weight against him.

Upon horses, who have a trick of turning short about suddenly, to the right for example, seperate the reins, taking one in each hand: leave the right one quite loose, and pull the left one, stretching out your hand from the horse to the left, and forwards. If the horse still resists, use your left leg, and spur; and so *vice versâ*, 'till he turns to the left. CHAP.

CHAP IX.

Several remarks and hints on shoeing, feeding, management of horses, &c. &c.

I Do not by any means intend to enter here largely on the many systems of shoeing; it would enlarge this treatise too much, and extend the object of it beyond the bounds I have prescribed to it, and to myself: as feet differ, so should shoes accordingly, but as it happens unfortunately for us, that the farriers belonging to the army, for want of proper education, due inspection, and encouragement, are void of all real skill, and knowledge in their profession, and have minds, in short, quite uncultivated, it is absolutely necessary to lay down only such rules, as are plain, general and invariable, and the strictest discipline must be enforced to make them all observed and followed most religiously. I do not however despair of seeing in time some intelligent farriers properly instructed; and when such are formed, and not 'till then, the number of them in regiments should be increased: It would even be much better to have none at all, 'till such a reformation is brought about. One man cannot properly shoe more than forty horses; at present we have only one to a troop of fifty-five, in time of war, besides bat-horses, and all others belonging to officers, sutlers, carriages, servants, &c. There should also be one forge-cart at least appropriated to each squadron, and a third for the latter-mentioned purposes: but they must not be like our present ones, which are made so heavy and with such low wheels, that they employ a great number of horses, ruin most of them, and after all, seldom get up to their respective regiments in right time, even in good roads, and never in bad ones. And I may say, that 'tis lucky they do not, for upon experience one finds fewer horses lame, during the absence of farriers, than when they are present. They should be built upon two wheels only, and those very high: The cart must be covered, and have partitions in it for the forge, bellows, tools, charcoal, &c. All these things must be so contrived, as to be easily taken out of the cart, and worked on the ground. This sort of forge-cart never sticks, and is always able to keep up with the regiments on any marches: it requires but few horses, and spoils none. I have one for my own use, made by the Hanoverian train,

which

which is drawn eafily by two horfes. For regiments, the carts muft be fomewhat larger, and more fubftantial, and would require three horfes. I doubt not, but an Englifh workman would improve upon them, as to ftrength and lightnefs, as well as convenience; tho' the cart I have, is very well conftructed, and anfwers well every neceffary purpofe.

Phyfic and a butteris in well-informed hands would not be fatal; but in the manner we are now provided with farriers, they muft be quite banifhed. Whoever lets his farrier, groom, or coachman, ever even mention any thing more than water-gruel, a clyfter, or a little bleeding, and that too very feldom; or pretend to talk of the nature of feet, of the feat of lameneffes, fickneffes, or their cures, may be certain to find himfelf very fhortly, and very abfurdly, quite on foot. It is incredible what tricking knaves moft ftable-people are, and what daring attempts they will make to gain an afcendant over their mafters, in order to have their own foolifh projects complied with. In fhoeing, for example, I have more than once known, that for the fake of eftablifhing their own ridiculous and pernicious fyftem, when their mafters have differed from it, they have, on purpofe, lamed horfes, and imputed the fault to the fhoes, after having in vain tried, by every fort of invention and lies, to difcredit the ufe of them. How the method of fuch people be commendable, whofe arguments, as well as practice, are void of common fenfe? If your horfe's foot be bad and brittle, they advife you to cover it with a very heavy fhoe; the confequence of which procceding is evident: for how fhould the foot, which before could fcarce carry itfelf, be able afterwards to carry fuch an additional weight, which is ftuck on moreover with a multitude of nails, the holes of which tear and weaken the hoof? If the foot is cut or hurt, one doctor fays, load it, by way of cover, with all you can: his conceited opponent as wifely counfels you to let the horfe walk bare upon the fore. The only fyftem all thefe fimpletons feem to agree in, is to fhoe in general with exceffive heavy, and clumfy ill-fhaped fhoes and very many nails, to the total deftruction of the foot. The cramps they annex, tend to deftroy the bullet, and the fhoes made in the fhape of a walnut-fhell, prevent the horfe's walking

walking upon the firm bafis, which nature has given him for that end, thereby oblige him to ftumble and fall, and of courfe from their fhape tear out the nails and ruin the hoof. Feet once got thoroughly out of fhape, by the cat walnut-fhell, or other ill-fhaped fhoes, are fometimes irrecoverable, and almoft always very difficult to correct; for horn being of a flexible nature, by being confined in a mould, will retain the fhape impreffed upon it by a bad fnaped fhoe, which never admits of the natural tread of the foot. The beft way, when a horfe is thus circumftanced, is to pare his feet down almoft to the quick, and fhort at the toe, and to turn him out without fhoes into fome foft grafs ground 'till the feet grow again before he is fhod. They totally pare away alfo, and lay bare the infide of the animal's foot with their deteftible butteris, which muft caufe narrow heels, becaufe the hard outfide of the foot will of courfe prefs in, when it finds no refiftance, the infide being cut away, and they afterwards put on very long fhoes, whereby the foot is hindered from having any preffure at all upon the heels, which preffure otherwife might ftill perchance, notwithftanding their dreadful cutting, keep the heels properly open, and the foot in good order. The frog

frog should never be cut out; but as it will sometimes become ragged, it must be cleaned every now and then, and the ragged pieces cut off with a knife. In one kind of foot indeed a considerable cutting away must be allowed of, but not of the frog; I mean that very high feet must be cut down to a proper height; because if they were not, the frog, tho' not cut, would still be so far above the ground, as not to have any bearing on it, whereby the great tendon must inevitably be damaged, and consequently the horse would go lame.

The weight of shoes must greatly, wholly indeed, depend on the quality and hardness of the iron. If the iron be very good, it will not bend; and in this case, the shoes cannot possibly be made too light; care however must be taken, that they be of a thickness so as not to bend; for bending would force out the nails, and ruin the hoof. That part of the shoe, which is next the horse's heel, must be narrower than any other, (as is seen in the draught) that stones may be thereby prevented from getting under it, and sticking there; which otherwise would be the case; because the iron, when it advances inwardly

beyond

BREAKING HORSES, &c.

beyond the bearing of the foot, forms a cavity, wherein stones being lodged would remain, and by pressing against the foot, lame the horse. Broad webbed shoes are very absurd things. Nothing more is wanted, than just iron enough to protect the outward crust of the foot, and to prevent its breaking. The nails in all shoes must, on account of the natural shape of the foot, be driven slanting a little towards the extreme edges of the foot. Any partial pressure towards the inward edge of the shoe, must of course, in a broad webbed shoe, loosen the nails, and consequently tear and damage the foot, supposing even the iron of the shoe good enough not to bend. This inconvenience of tearing out the nails, &c. great as it is, is the best which can happen in this case; for, if the iron was to bend, it would press against the inward part of the foot, and lame the horse just as much as if the shoe had not been bevilled off at all in the proper place, for the picker to be put in, in order to clean out stones, gravel, &c. Making a groove round the edges of shoes, if the iron is not very good, may cause a partial yielding there; but if the iron is good, a groove is very useful, to protect the heads of the nails. Farriers should always examine a foot before they shoe it, make the shoe, and pierce the holes for the nails further from, or nearer to, the edges of the foot accordingly, as they find the foot requires. The holes for the nails should always be pierced slanting rather outwards. The best way to forge shoes, in respect to the nails, is to make the holes for the nails at twice, with two different instruments: first on the outside of the shoe punch a place, not quite through the shoe, big enough to receive, and cover the head of the nail, when driven in: next punch a smaller hole, from the center of the abovementioned larger one, for the blade of the nail, quite through the shoe: thus the nails are well driven in, protected, and can not be pushed by use too much into the foot, but always keep their firm, proper place, full as well as, nay better than in a grooved shoe in case the iron should not be perfectly good. All shoes should be a little broader at the extremities towards the heels, than elsewhere, except the foot spreads of itself too much at the heel, which is seldom the case; if the horse cuts, they must not be made so: the reason why they should generally be broader there is, that they encourage the foot to grow, spread properly, and therefore prevent narrow heels. It must always

ways be remembered, that where the web grows narrow towards the heel, the feat of the shoe must nevertheless keep its usual proper equal breadth within, otherwise the horse's foot would not have its equal proper basis, or *appui*, and the shoe would get into the foot, and require frequent removals, which are great inconveniences. The part of the shoe, which the horse walks upon, should be quite flat, and the inside of it likewise; only just space enough being left next the foot, to put in a picker, (which ought to be used every time the horse comes into the stable, and often on marches) and also to prevent the shoe's pressing upon the sole. In snowy weather, it is particularly necessary to pick and clean the feet very often, on marches; otherwise the snow soon grows very hard in the feet, makes the horse slip about very much, and hurts him almost as much as large stones in the feet would do. Four nails on each side, hold better than a greater number, and keep the hoof in a far better state. The toe of the horse must be cut short, and nearly square, (the angles only just rounded off) nor must any nails be driven there; this method prevents much stumbling, especially in descents, and serves by throwing nourishment to the heels, to strengthen them;

on them the horse should in some measure walk, and the shoe be made of a proper length accordingly: by this means narrow heels are prevented, and many other good effects produced. Many people drive a nail at the toe, but it is an absurd practice. Leaving room to drive one there causes the foot to be of an improper length, and moreover that part of the hoof is naturally so brittle, that the nail there seldom stays in, but tears out, and damages the hoof. That my directons for shoeing a proper length may be the more clear and intelligible, I have annexed a draught of a foot shod of a proper length, standing on a plain surface, and with it a draught of the right kind of shoe. *(Plate* 16. No. 1. the interior part of the shoe next the foot, and No. 2. the exterior part, which rests on the ground.) Most farriers make shoes thicker at the heels, than at the toes, especially for hard working horses: the great folly of doing so is very easy to be seen, for horse-shoes always wear out sooner at the toe, than any where else; consequently the toe rather requires more substance, than any other part. In some farriers shops the anvils are concave, and the hammers convex, so that it is almost impossible a well shaped flat shoe should be made there. Place the shoe both ways on a flat surface, and it is surprizing how faulty the form of it is generally.

La Fosse's tips, or half shoes, are particularly useful for feet whose crust is too weak to bear nails towards the hinder parts of the foot, and whose heels have a tendency to grow narrow. Pity it is that they require being frequently removed.

In wet, spungy, and soft ground, where the foot sinks in, the pressure upon the heels is of course greater, than on hard ground; and so indeed it should be upon all accounts. The hinder feet must be treated in the same manner as the fore ones, and the shoes the same: except in hilly and slippery countries, where they may not improperly be turned up a little behind: but turning up the fore-shoes is very seldom, I am convinced, of any service, and is very prejudicial to the fore legs, especially to the bullets. In very greasy, wet, or loose kind of slippery soils indeed, where the ground easily gives way, and lets the foot in, without however holding it in very strongly, turning up before may be useful, but in a hard country, where the foot can not enter the ground, cramps before are very hurtful, and quite useless; the tendon being by them elevated, and therefore constantly straining itself for want of a basis to rest on, they endamage the sinews very much, and cause wind-galls, lameness, swellings on the bullet, and weaknesses, &c. almost as much as the walnut-shell shaped shoe, which is held in such high esteem by bad farriers, and their ignorant stable followers. In descending hills, unless in the above-mentioned kind of soils, cramps on the fore feet are apt to throw horses down, by stopping the fore legs, out of their proper basis and natural bearing, when the hinder ones are rapidly pressed; which unavoidably must be the case, and consequently cannot but push the horse upon his nose. With them on a plain surface, a horse's foot is always thrown forwards on the toe, out of its proper bearing, which is very liable to make the horse stumble. The notion of their utility in going up hills is a false one. In ascending, the toe is the first part of the foot, which bears on, and takes hold of the ground, whether the horse draws, or carries; and consequently the business is almost done, before the part, where the cramps are, comes to the ground. Ice nails are preferable to any thing to prevent slipping, as also to help horses up hill, the most forward ones taking hold of the ground early, considerably before the heels touch the ground: they must be so made,

BREAKING HORSES, &c.

as to be, when driven in, about a quarter of an inch above the shoe; and also have four sides ending at the top in a point. They are of great service to prevent slipping on all kinds of places, and by means of them a horse is not thrown out of his proper basis. They must be made of very good iron; if they are not, the heads of them will be perpetually breaking off, which will not happen, if the iron is good, and the nails are well made, of the above-mentioned shape and size. Making them with higher heads, would render them liable to break off, and answer no purpose whatever. When, in the not long ago mentioned kinds of grounds, cramps on the fore feet are used, they should be small, and the heads of the nails should stand up in the manner of the ice nails, but not quite so high, above the shoe, by which the foot and the tendons would always have their proper bearing. These nails may be also used without any cramps. By putting a fresh nail every now and then on the shoe, as wanted, all wished for ends are obtained, and no bad effects ensue. I know that I am fighting against a very strong, though very unreasonable prejudice. Let this method be tried only, and

compared

compared fairly on experience with others; and not immediately laid aside, if, in slippery weather, a horse thus shod should now and then slip. In some weather, and on some ground, any horse any how shod, may sometimes chance to fall. There is unluckily no absolute specific against accidental falling in any shoes yet discovered. I have tried all methods, and find the above-mentioned one the nearest to perfection: this sort of shoe and nails, when well made and fixed properly, being the firmest basis, and best hold I ever knew. I do not recommend ice nails at all times: in certain weather, (the greatest part of the year indeed) the ground is in a condition which does not require any. From the race-horse to the cart-horse, the same system of shoeing should be observed: the size, thickness, and weight of them only should differ: the shoe of a race-horse must of course be lighter than that of a saddle-horse; that of a saddle-horse lighter than that of a troop, coach, draught, or bat horse; and these last more so than a cart, waggon, or artillery horse. A saddle-horse's shoe should weigh thirteen ounces and a half; that of a coach, or draught-horse one pound and three ounces: the nails for the former one ounce per dozen; those for the latter one

ounce

BREAKING HORSES, &c.

ounce and three quarters. Much the easiest way, and in general the best, is to use a narrow-webbed shoe, all over of one equal breadth both within and without, with the holes for the nails exactly in the middle: with little or no art, such a shoe is made out of a narrow bar of iron: it must necessarily be always narrow, for there can be no bevel in it, or it would press upon and hurt the inside of the foot: it has one great advantage over all other shoes, that stones cannot lodge in it. At present all shoes in general are too *heavy:* if the iron is good, shoes need not be so thick, as they are now generally made. With exceedingly heavy loads, such as large cannon, in hilly, slippery countries, and in the bad seasons of the year, the thiller horse should be turned up both before and behind, with three cramps on each shoe; one in the middle part of the toe of the shoe; which in going up hill would help the horse much in his first force to draw his weight after him. I mean this only for a thiller horse, and in certain countries, and weather, when the foot can enter the ground, so that the elevation given to the shoe has no inconvenience attending it. The utmost severity ought to be inflicted upon all those who clap shoes on hot: this

unpar-

unpardonable lazinefs of farriers in making feet thus fit fhoes, inftead of fhoes fitting feet, dries up the hoofs, and utterly deftroys them. It has happened, that the fole has been fo much heated by a hot fhoe, that a horfe has been moft dangeroufly lamed, and fome have even loft their lives by it. Shoes fhould be always made and fitted before the holes are pierced. The fhoes in England at prefent, that are contrived with the moft fenfe, are what they call plates for the race-horfes at New-Market: I do not fay, that they are perfect, but they are nearer the truth, than any others I know; nor are they fubftantial enough for common ufe, though fufficiently fo for the turf.

It is fometimes eafy to cure horfes of cutting by fhoeing, but far from always: nine times in ten their doing it proceeds from their turning out their toes. Colts generally graze with one foot ftretched out, which refts on the infide, by which the infide is worn down; this makes the toe grow outwards, and the colt becomes crooked from the fetlock downwards: the cutting then generally proceeds from the infide being lower than the outfide; the

outfide

BREAKING HORSES, &c.

outſide therefore muſt be frequently pared down, and the inſide not. If the foot is ſuch as will not bear cutting, the ſhoe muſt be made thicker on the inſide web, than on the outſide one, from the heel to the toe, and every time the horſe is ſhod, the ſhoe muſt be turned a little inwards, and the outſide of the hoof raſped off, 'till the foot becomes quite ſtraight by degrees. Bar-ſhoes can never be good, or uſeful, but juſt for a very little time, to cover ſome damaged part of the foot, if the poor horſe can not be ſpared from work, 'till he is cured.

'Tis ſtrange, that there ſhould be ſo many ridiculous and abſurd methods of ſhoeing, when it is ſo manifeſt, that a ſmall ſhare of common-ſenſe, with a moment's reflection upon the ſtructure of a horſe's foot, cannot but ſuggeſt the proper one. Frequent removals of ſhoes are detrimental and tear the foot, but ſometimes they are very neceſſary: this is an inconvenience, which half-ſhoes are liable to, (though excellent in ſeveral other reſpects) for the end of the ſhoe being very ſhort is apt to work ſoon into the foot, and conſequently muſt then be moved. Soldiers ſhould always carry two ſpare ſhoes

Q   with

with them, on the upper end and outward fide of each holfter pipe, with fome nails. Some fhould carry a hammer, others a pair of pinchers, others a butteris, and all be taught how to fix on a fhoe. The weight of thefe things properly divided is trifling. The ufe of them would be foon found on fervice, particularly with light troops, and on detachments, where farriers cannot be prefent.

The common practice of ftuffing feet with dung is a very bad one, for the dung contains a rotting quality in it: clay and hog's lard, well mixed together, is much better for that purpofe. As to hoof ointment, none is better than that made of one pound of neat's foot oil, one pound of turpentine, and ten ounces of bees-wax. Greafing and ftopping, though good for moft feet, are not fo for all: weak fpungy crufts and foles are the worfe for it: fuch muft be kept dry. Strong feet muft be often wetted, greafed, and ftopped, and the cruft kept down low, or they will fall in by the ftrong preffure of the cruft, and caufe narrow heels. When horfes are hot, the water with which their feet are wafhed fhould be lukewarm: if the heels are cracked, thofe parts fhould be wafhed with

with milk and water, and a little brandy in it, made a little warm. Mr. CLARKE, in his excellent treatise upon shoeing and feet, insists, that oil, greasy stuffings, and ointments agree but with few hoofs, that they stop the natural perspiration; and that frequent washings with water, moisture, and coolness, keep them in a much more perfect state. The experience I have had since I saw his book, convinces me that he is right in general: the natural and superior benefit which feet and hoofs receive at grass from the dew, rains and moisture of the earth, is a proof of it: and on the other hand we see, that race-horses, particularly at New-Market, where they are always exercised on a dry, close turf, and where they drink out of troughs, round which there is no water for them to stand in, are subject to a variety of diseases in the feet, and hoofs, though they are kept constantly greased.

The methods of treating and keeping horses in other respects, are as various, and for the generality as inconsistent with reason, as those of shoeing are; but a little consideration would (in most common cases at least) direct people right in both. One pampers his cattle, with a view of strengthening them; and afterwards, by way of correction, he pours down drugs into them without thought or measure: another lets no air at all into his stable; from whence his horses inevitably catch cold, when they stir out of it, and are rotted, if they stay in it, by bad corrupted air: a third, equally wise, leaves his stable open, and his cattle exposed to the wind and weather at all times, whether his horses or the weather be hot or cold, and frequently too even in wind-draughts, whilst they are in a sweat. All these different notions and practices are alike attended with destruction to horses; as also are the many extravagances that prevail in the same contradictory extremes, with regard to coverings. But in answer to all these foolish systems, reason plainly suggests to us, that proper wholesome food, a well-tempered circulation of sweet air, moderate and constant exercise, with due care, and suitable cloathing, as weather and occasions may require, will never fail to preserve horses sound and in health.

After working, and at night of course, as also in lamenesses, and sicknesses, 'tis good for horses to stand on litter; it also promotes staleing, &c. At other times it is
a bad

BREAKING HORSES, &c.

a bad cuſtom; the conſtant uſe of it heats and makes the feet tender, and cauſes ſwelled legs: moreover it renders the animal delicate. Swelled legs may frequently be reduced to their proper natural ſize by taking away the litter only, which, in ſome ſtables, where ignorant grooms, and farriers govern, would be a great ſaving of phyſic and bleeding, beſides ſtraw. I have ſeen by repeated experiments, legs ſwell, and unſwell, by leaving litter, or taking it away, like mercury in a weather-glaſs.

It is of the greateſt conſequence for horſes to be kept clean, regularly fed, and as regularly exerciſed: but whoever chuſes to ride in the way of eaſe and pleaſure, without any fatigue on horſeback, or in ſhort does not like to carry his horſe, inſtead of his horſe's carrying him, muſt not ſuffer his horſe to be exerciſed by a groom, ſtanding up on his ſtirrups, holding himſelf on by means of the reins, and thereby hanging his whole dead weight on the horſe's mouth, to the entire deſtruction of all that is good, ſafe or pleaſant about the animal. No horſe's paces can be perfect, nor can he be agreeable, or indeed quite ſafe, unleſs his mouth has been made, and his body ſuppled to

a cera certain degree, so as to be balanced in the rider's hand. A horse's head should be kept high: when it is low, the animal can not be well balanced; for the fore parts being low, and weighing forwards, the hinder parts must of course be high: the fore parts are naturally much more loaded than the hinder ones, though of a less strong construction. The rider ought to know as much as his horse, at least; for, without art, it is impossible to preserve that *union*, and that *together*, if I may so express myself, which are equally pleasing, and necessary: a man on a totally uninstructed horse, or an ill-instructed one, rides, as it were, upon a coach pole.

A great quantity of hay, especially that which is taken from water meadows, or any low and swampy ground, being of a foggy nature, is not good for horses; it hurts their wind very much: it may serve indeed for cart-horses, and for such troop-horses (few of such, thank God, now remain) who are meant for no other use; but to roll on slowly with a fat fellow, full of beer, upon them; who, to the shame of the service, with the badge of soldiership on his back, is a more stupid and lazy animal, than what

he

he is mounted upon, which to its misfortune is rendered so by the fluggifhnefs of its rider. But troops, who are really deftined for fervice, and to be ufeful, muft be active and in wind; the very training them only, to what is abfolutely neceffary, requires that they fhould be fo, more, or lefs, according to the different intents and purpofes they may be defigned for.

Upon fervice, the allowance of all kinds of forage, whenever there is a poffibility of fupplying it, is fufficient; but fometimes it cannot be procured for a long while together: befides which misfortune, it is very often moft fhamefully and carelefsly wafted; not to mention, that commiffaries in general feldom furnifh out the due quantity or quality of any thing, which they have agreed and engaged for, and are moft amply paid for,

At home, our horfes are crammed and ruined with overmuch hay, and the allowance of corn is fcanty. A kind of mill, not to grind corn, but only juft to crack and bruife it a little, is fo ufeful, that no regiment fhould ever march without one. Every grain of it goes to nourifhment; none is to be found in the dung; and three feeds of it go further

than

than four as commonly given, which have not been in the mill. Cut wheaten straw, and a little hay too sometimes mixed with it, is excellent food: to a quartern of corn put the same quantity of cut straw, and now and then if a horse is very lean, but not otherwise, about half a one of hay, and let them all be well mingled together; and as chopped straw is generally exceedingly dry, sprinkle a little water upon the feed in the manger. This proportion of chopped straw may seem great, but considering the lightness of it, it is not such in reality. It obliges horses to chew their meat, and is many other ways of use. The quantity of horses food must be proportioned to their size, work, make, appetite, &c.; yet, in regiments it is necessary to fix, and follow some kind of general rule in respect to it. Four of these feeds as above-mentioned, with ten or twelve pounds of hay per day, will be sufficient for most horses on almost on all occasions, except at the piquet late in the year in bad weather; then they should be almost always feeding on something, or other; and if they have no corn, they will consume near forty pounds a day of hay, allowing for some waste, which is unavoidable, especially on bad ground, and in windy weather.

BREAKING HORSES, &c.

weather. When the forage confifts of unthrafhed ftraw only, eight-and-twenty, or thirty pounds of it for each horfe will do very well, efpecially, if the cutting-box is made ufe of, as it always fhould be. Whenever forage is fcarce, the beft method is to have every thing cut, and given to the horfes every two hours, in nofe-bags, or deep canvafs troughs, fo that the wind may blow none away. Even in time of peace at home, the cutting-box fhould be ufed conftantly. The allowance at home cannot afford fo much, neither indeed is fo much neceffary, when troops are not on fervice. The exercife horfes take at home, though it fhould perhaps be greater, and more conftant, than it is in fome corps, does not require it. A matter of the greateft confequence, though few attend to it, is to feed horfes according to their work, and never to fuffer them to pafs the day quite ftill, without fome motion at leaft. When the work is hard, food fhould be in plenty; when it is otherwife, the food fhould be diminifhed immediately; the hay particularly. Horfes fhould be turned loofe fomewhere, or walked about every day, when they do not work, particularly after hard exercife. Swelled legs, phyfic, &c. will be faved by thefe means, and many diftempers avoided.

I cannot mention the word piquet, without saying something on our pernicious cuftom of cutting horfe's tails entirely off, the inconvenience of which is very glaring in many inftances; but in none more, or more ferioufly fo, than at piquets on fervice, when in hot weather, and in ground where there are many flies. I have often feen our horfes, with meat before them, fretting, fweating, kicking about, laming one another, and fo plagued with flies for want of tails to brufh them away, that they did not eat at all, and fo grew out of condition, whilft the neighbouring foreign regiments on the fame ground brufh'd off the flies with their tails, were cool, quiet, and fed at their eafe, and improved. Since that time indeed our cavalry has been ordered to recruit only long tails, and tis to be hoped the nation will follow the example, though old cuftoms, even the worft, I know, are hard to be got the better of. That of cutting off horfes tails, ears, and other extremities, is a very old noted one indeed amongft us in England; for fo long ago as the year 747, a canon was, by order of Pope Gregory the fecond, in a letter to St. Auguftine, exprefly made at an ecclefiaftical court in Yorkfhire, to abolifh, amongft other cruel cuftoms, fo barbarous

BREAKING HORSES, &c.

barous a practice. On duty and marches long tails are very easily tied up properly, and look very well: a nag-tail indeed, suffered to grow a little, protects a horse pretty well. All sorts of grains are foggy feeding, and though they plump up the body, they do not give a wholesome and sound fat: bran too, is not solid food, and is only now and then to be allowed, when horses are heated, to refresh, and open them, if the case requires it.

Whenever hay is put and left in the racks, it should be well cleaned and freed from dust, and not given in too large quantities: in this respect 'tis, like water, much more beneficial, when supplied in small quantities at a time. When a good deal is given at a time, horses spoil, and do not eat the greatest part of it very often, by having blown upon it a good while. A proper quantity of it should be given at twice; a little in the morning before watering, and the rest sometime after they have done their work in the evening. Nothing but good clean wheaten-straw should be left at night in the racks, when the stables are shut up, and the horses left to rest. If hay is left for them, they will frequently stand up to feed almost all night, lie down but little, and take scarcely any rest. A little straw sometimes in the racks during the day time is also proper.

Both before, and after working, horses should be turned about with their croupes to the manger for about an hour. 'Tis a common, but a great error, and very detrimental to horses, to gallop them immediately after drinking; what stable-men call warming the water in their bellies: they ought to be moved only gently. Upon the whole, a very lean horse, and a very fat horse are both in a manner useless to a certain degree: a rough coat is no good symptom; but the means of making it fine should not be by dint of heat and covering, but by dressing and due care. It is of the greatest consequence to a horse's health, that he should always be well rubbed down, and cleaned. Laziness is the true reason why grooms cover horses so much, and keep stables so hot, though they disguise it under the pretence of thinking it wholesome, which indeed however the most ignorant of them really do. A horse when absolutely ruined by over heat will nevertheless very often have a very fine good looking coat.

It

BREAKING HORSES, &c.

It is a duty very requisite, and incumbent upon officers, to be as constant, exact, and frequent in going up and down the lines in camp, as through the stables in quarters; and it is likewise adviseable for every one to visit often his own stables, to inspect and superintend the management of the horses. No trimming with cizars should be permitted; but whatever rough hairs appear, should be taken off by dressing. The inside particularly of the ears should never be trimmed, but always kept cleaned: nature has placed hairs within them for reasons very obvious: when they are cut away, dust and insects frequently get into the ears, incomode horses very much, and sometimes cause a serious ailment in those parts. As great inconveniences often happen from horses getting loose, I have affixed a draught and description of the most effectual halter I know of; *(Pla.* 17.) and indeed the only one I have found upon trial, that is capable of preventing it.

This halter has no throat-band, or rather it has, in a manner, two, which are fixed, and begin at No. 1. They cross at 2, are fixed again and end at 3. The nose band is also sowed on at 3. The place 2, where the throat-
bands

bands meet, is a flat button, which is placed, when the halter is well put on, juſt under the ganaches, (the channel between the two jaw-bones.) The chains, ropes, or leathers, No. 4, which tie the horſe in the ſtable, are alſo fixed at 3. No. 5, a ſingle cord or leather; if the horſe is only faſtened with one, which will be as effectual as two.

As horſes are generally more ſupple to the left, than to the right, owing to their being, from their earlieſt youth, more handled on that ſide, than the other, they ſhould not only be led with the left hand, in order that they may bend rather to the right, than to the left; but all collars, caveſſons, girts, bridles, bridoons, pillar cords, &c. ſhould be made for the ſame reaſon, to buckle, and unbuckle on the right ſide. Horſes often hang themſelves in their halters, and frequently hurt themſelves a good deal by it: the beſt remedy for ſuch accidents is merely to keep the hurt clean by waſhing it with lukewarm water with ſome brandy in it, and every now and then to ſupple the part with a little green ointment, ſuch as mallows, &c. boiled to a certain conſiſtency, and mixed with ſweet oil. When

BREAKING HORSES, &c.

When horses are out of cafe, have buttons broke out about them, their legs fwell, and their coats ftare, and there is not time (nor perhaps an abfolute neceffity for it) to phyfic them, a rowel, and two ounces of the following powder, given every morning for twenty, or thirty days, in wetted corn, fo that none can be blown away, are of great fervice: the powder to be compofed of one pound of liver of antimony, half a pound of fulphur, and a quarter of a pound of nitre, mixed well together: if the horfe has a cough, make it into balls, with flour and treacle, or any fuch kind of thing.

A common complaint amongft troop-horfes is broken-wind, which is chiefly occafioned by ftuffing them with too much hay; and often by hurrying them too violently after drinking, and after their coming at firft from grafs. There is no fovereign remedy for broken-wind; but the greateft palliative I know of, is this following receipt of lime-water, which is oftener of fervice if continued long, or rather always indeed than any other remedy I know of, owing probably not only to the good effects of the lime, but alfo to the fmall quantity of liquid the horfes take;

for

for very few will ever drink plentifully of this water, and many will go several days without drinking at all, before they will even taste it: the horse must eat no hay at all, and only have wheaten straw in the rack: this water must be used too when mashes are given, and on every other occasion: in short no other water is ever to be given in any shape whatever: 'tis made thus---Take two pounds of quick lime, and put to it twelve gallons of water; mix it over night, stirring it for a long time together, and pouring the water on very gradually 'till the ebullition is over; then leave it to settle for use the next day. If a chalybeate spring is at hand, the lime-water will be much the better for being made of it, instead of any common water. This medicine causes no inconvenience, or impediment, and does not prevent the horse from working as usual. A horse, whose wind is suspicious, should immediately be put on lime-water, and never drink more than a gallon or five quarts in a day, and no horse should drink more than double that quantity, that too at two or three different times. Three pints of warm milk from the cow, night and morning, will sometimes prevent horses heaving, or coughing for a short time, even in tolerably smart exercise; but as

the

the advantages arising from the milk are of so short a duration, this method may, with reason, be looked upon more as a dealer's trick to sell off a broken-winded horse by, than as a remedy. Farriers generally send horses touched in the wind to grass, which, opening them, at first seems to do them good, but, when they are taken into the stable again, and put for some time on hard meat, they are always worse than before, and the distemper more rooted in.

Worms are so common, and so troublesome a distemper, that I can not omit saying something of them here. Horses, who look out of order, are frequently so owing to worms; that must be examined into always immediately. Give fasting, and let the horse fast three or four hours after it, a quart of beef brine every morning for three or four days. The brine alone will often cure entirely, a purge being given the day after all the brine is taken; a clyster should be given over night, before the purge. If from one ounce and a half to two ounces of Æthiop's mineral in a bolus is given the day after all the brine is taken, and a day before the purge, the cure will be still more certain. You'll see the dead worms in the horse's dung.

A running at the nose, with a cough, and other symptoms, known by the name of *the distemper*, is so frequent, and so ill treated by farriers, that I can not help giving some directions for the treatment of it. Give frequent clysters, keep a rowel or two running for some time, and, if the illness be violent, and attended by a fever, give James's fever powders for three nights running, the first night three papers, the second night two papers, and the third night one paper. No bleeding at first. Then give, for four days running, two ounces of nitre, and afterwards an ounce and a half a day for some time. Poultice from the very beginning under and about the throat, with bread, milk, and lard, made pretty hot; if any thing hard thereabouts grows soft, and does not break of itself, open it with a lancet, and cleanse it thoroughly. As soon as the running at the nose ceases, and not before, give very gentle exercise, and, if the cough then still remains, bleed very little at a time, but frequently, 'till it ceases. Keep the horse by no means cold, but let him have fresh air. He must not be moved 'till the running at the nose ceases. Don't physic, but continue the ounce and a half of nitre for three weeks at least, and give two or three times a week,

for

for as long as is found neceffary, a drink made of liquorice root, ftones of raifins bruis'd, and figs dry'd, of each two ounces, and one ounce of maiden-hair; boil them together in a quart of water, 'till reduced to a pint, then add fyrup of balfam, cold drawn linfeed oil, of each two ounces, and one ounce of nitre. This drink not to be given 'till the running at the nofe ceafes. If the diftemper is exceedingly flight, James's powders, may be omitted. If the tefticles fwell, ufe cooling things, fuch as warm milk and water, marfh-mallows, &c. but above all things, don't neglect to fufpend them in a fling. Keep the nofe and noftrils very clean, by wafhing them frequently with warm water. Feed with mafhes only, and continue the poultice 'till the running of the nofe has ceafed two or three days. Then the covering about the throat muft be taken off by degrees, a little at a time.

Greafy and fwelled legs being a very common diftemper in troop horfes, I fhall fet down the following very good receipt for the cure of it:---Take falt-petre two ounces and two drams, the fame quantity of venice turpentine, one ounce and four drams of flour of brimftone, diapente fix drams; mix the whole together with a fufficient quantity of liquorice powder, make it into balls, and give it to the horse fasting in the morning; he must not eat for two hours after taking it, nor drink for five or six hours, and then the water must be warmish; he must be kept warm, and have gentle walking exercise the next day; this dose must be repeated twice, or more, as required, with an interval of three days between each dose.

The following manner of treating the grease is also a very good one.---As medicines to be given inwardly, take of powdered resin one ounce and a half; of salt of tartar, and sal prunell, each six drams; spirit of turpentine, enough to make it into a ball. The proper dose for a large horse is three ounces: it should be given when first made up, or else the salt of tartar will make its escape. This will operate as a diuretic two days, during which time the horse is to have plenty of scalded bran, plenty of warm water, and gentle walking. The third and fourth morning, he is to take a ball made of the following medicines. Take of foenugreek, aniseed, elecampane, turmerick, liquorice powder, diapente powdered, each equal parts; add to a pound of this powder two ounces of anisated balsam of sulphur,

sulphur, and honey enough to make it of a proper consistence: the dose of this ball to be of the size of a hen's egg: the diuretic ball is to be given in the morning; the day following nothing; the two succeeding mornings, the cordial ball; and so on 'till the diuretic ball has been given three times: the cordial ball to be continued every day after the third diuretic ball is given, 'till the horse is well.

As external applications,---if there be a swelling of the parts, they should be poulticed with warm rye meal, and milk, boiled to a proper consistence, which is to be renewed every day. When the swelling is gone, apply the following: take of honey two pounds and a half; of train oil, and powdered allum, each two pounds; boil them to a proper consistence: some of this to be spread on a linen rag, and applied to the parts: to be renewed once in forty-eight hours. The horse must not go out, when this medicine is applied. This will dry up the sores, and, if there is any scurf, or scab left, use the following mixture: take of the juice of houseleek one part; of very thick cream two parts; beat it up together into an ointment, and rub some of it every day on the parts affected.

Resin

Refin drink is alfo very good for fwelled legs. The following is alfo a good method of curing the greafe: pluck out the hairs clean, with pinchers, all about, and upon the greafed part. Then put on a turnip poultice, and leave it on twenty-four hours; then fpread a linen bandage with tar, and wrap it, not loofe, nor tight, round the part, and leave it on three or four days. Continue at the fame time, the balls, or refin drink, and take away fome blood once or twice, a little at a time.

When a horfe is lame, no matter where, grooms and farriers generally fay he is fo in the fhoulder, which is very feldom the cafe. If he really is fo, he will drag his toe on the ground, or move his legs circularly, more or lefs, according to the degree of the hurt; if he does not do it at all, he is not lame in the fhoulder. Every body who is in the leaft acquainted with the texture of a horfe, knows this to be true. When a horfe's lamenefs proceeds from any other caufe, from the knee downwards, one may generally know it by fome inflammation, or other fign, fuch as fwellings, tenderneffes, &c. One may generally fufpect with reafon fomething wrong in the feet, or coronary ring, owing chiefly to the common very bad method of managing feet. Running thrufhes are

are a common complaint, and though they are to be stopped, generally end in eating away the infide of the foot: Vitriol and water dry thefe thrufhes, and fo does a mixture of one-third fpirit of nitre, and two-thirds of fpirit of wine dabbed with a rag, and feveral other applications of that kind. When horfes, who are troubled with them, tread on a fharpifh ftone, the pain they feel from it is often fo great, that they fall down as if they were fhot. Sometimes a clumfy fellow, by negligence and aukwardnefs, which is oftener the cafe, than by any other accident, is the caufe of his horfe's falling, and breaking his knees. If any thing will make the hair come again, and probably of a right colour, burnt cork finely fifted, mixed with oil, and made into an ointment will do it; but if the horfe is grey, the burnt cork muft be omitted, and honey mixed up with the oil in lieu of it, becaufe the burnt cork, by caufing the hair to grow up of a darkifh colour, would disfigure a grey, or white horfe. Before the cork, and oil ointment is ufed, poultice the part with pounded turnips boil'd with milk, and mixed up with hog's lard, and a little friar's balfam; 'till there is no fwelling or irritation left. The poultice muft be put on frefh every twenty-four hours; the ointment muft be laid on very often, and the part muft be kept free from dirt.

For

For ſtrains of all kinds, ſoap, and camphor diſſolved into ſpirits of wine, and often well rubbed on the part, which muſt be afterwards covered with tow and warm pitch, are excellent. The tow thus ſtuck, and left on, keeps the injured part from cold, &c. and it is ſome time before it wears off: it is indeed a blemiſh for the time, but beſides being a good remedy in itſelf, it is otherwiſe of great uſe, as it puts it abſolutely out of the power of grooms and farriers to play any of their tricks, or for the latter to have any pretence whatſoever to be about the ſtables. It is a common cuſtom to give walking exerciſe to horſes who have ſprains, which is very pernicious; they ſhould not be ſtirred at all, if poſſible: abſolute reſt is the beſt remedy for them.

A blanket for each man carried under the ſaddle is of vaſt uſe to the horſe's back, as well as to the man on many occaſions. Every man ſhould have one.

Every troop ought to have a cutting-box belonging to it, and one man conſtantly employed in camp all day at it in chopping hay, ſtraw, &c. It is very eaſily carried about.

Forage, whatever it is, muſt not be cut too long, nor very ſhort,

short, but of such a length, that it may not, from its lightness, be blown up the horse's nostrils out of the nose-bag, or canvas trough. A lazy fellow at the cutting-box, if not watched, is very apt, by way of getting rid of his work soon, to cut it much too long.

The Germans wisely carry, upon all occasions whatever, every man a double feed of chopped straw and corn mixed together, which is never touched, but by express order of the commanding officer, and then too in such quantities, and at what time, he thinks fit to direct. It frequently happens upon long marches, and even sometimes when the troops stand still, that forage cannot be procured for some days together; then this practice, which I have just mentioned, in a short time gives strong and apparent proofs of its utility, by the preservation of their horse's good plight. It is the means of saving the lives of many horses, and helps, in cases of exigencies, to keep up the vigour of most of them. None but those, who have been eye-witnesses to the fact, can tell what harm a deficiency of forage, only for two days, does horses, especially in marches by night, and in bad weather: some are often disabled by it for the whole campaign, and some for ever after.

In the beginning of September, in our climates, green forage is no longer plenty on the ground. It would therefore be prudent from that time to make every man carry twenty pounds of spun hay, and afterwards later in the year a larger quantity. From about the twentieth of September, for example, or thereabouts, he might carry thirty pounds for the rest of the campaign, and, besides this hay, eight pounds of oats mixed with four pounds of cut wheaten straw, none of these to be ever touched, but by order of the commanding officer, and then in such quantity as he thinks fit. This method would often prevent troops from being in great want, and richly repay the horse for carrying the forage. As hay spoils by being kept twisted up for a long time together, it should be unspun, and given to the horses at the end of three days, and a fresh truss spun, and made up. If the campaign should last through the whole winter, this forage must be carried, 'till there is green forage enough on the ground the ensuing year, which may not be 'till late, in poor uncultivated countries, or those worn out by war. Whenever horses come out of quarters, where they have met with abundance, corn must be taken from them by degrees, if possible, and not all at once, be the season, and the country they take the field

BREAKING HORSES, &c.

in ever so good. For a considerable time horses will do very well in the field without corn, if, on coming out of quarters, they are not weaned from it too suddenly, and the weather, and green forage is tolerably good; but late in the year, when the weather grows bad, and horses are obliged to go a great way for forage, some corn is absolutely necessary.

In fetching forage, especially from any distance, the trusses should be very well made and fixed, and no men suffered to ride on them; the weight of both being immense. I have very often seen trusses of three hundred weight, which without a man on it, is a very heavy load. Laziness and custom has made some people imagine that a truss of forage cannot be carried without a man on it, but it is not so by any means, if the trusses are well made, and properly fixed. These, and many other precautions and care, in matters, seemingly perhaps little and trifling, ought to be deemed, (as they really are) equally as necessary for preserving a regiment in the condition it ought to be for its own credit, and the public service, as a just distribution of rewards and punishments. These, and such-like attentions should no more be dispensed with, than that an officer of each
troop

troop should constantly visit every horse of that troop daily in their lines, cantonments, or quarters; and especially too, and without delay, after fatiguing marches, and foul weather: but if this care be intrusted to a quarter-master, who is already over-loaded, not only with his own, but often with the whole business of the officers, beyond a possibility of executing half of it; and if he likewise, (being indeed in some measure compelled to it) shuffle off his burden, all he can, upon the serjeants and corporals, what else can be expected, but that the same spirit of idleness and disregard will diffuse itself throughout the whole corps? Hence no duty would be compleatly and essentially performed; none in the stables or camp with respect to the horses, accoutrements, &c. no regularity in cooking; no care to see the men well dried after wet service; in short, no serious attention to numberless other necessary articles of discipline, &c. whereby a regiment would most infamously fall to ruin, and be very soon rendered unfit for service.

THE END.

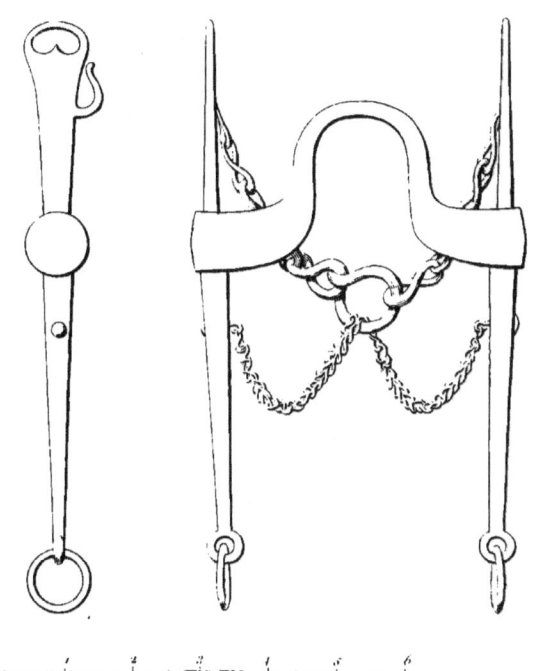

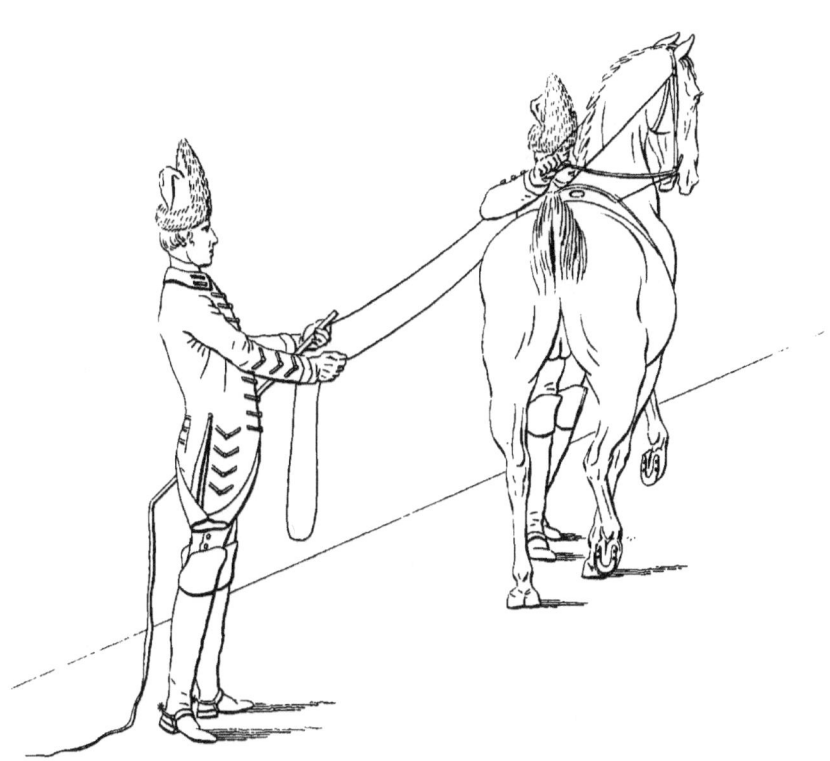

Pla. 9

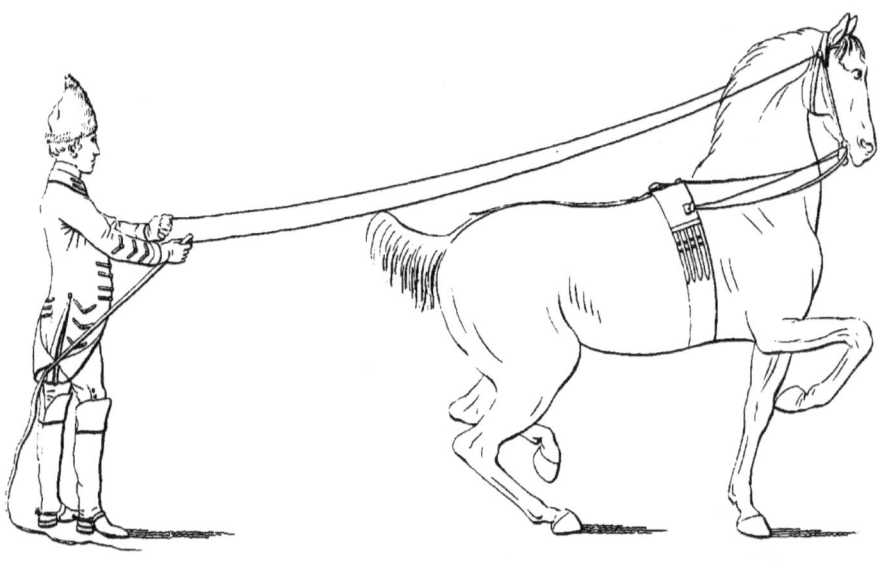

Pla. II.

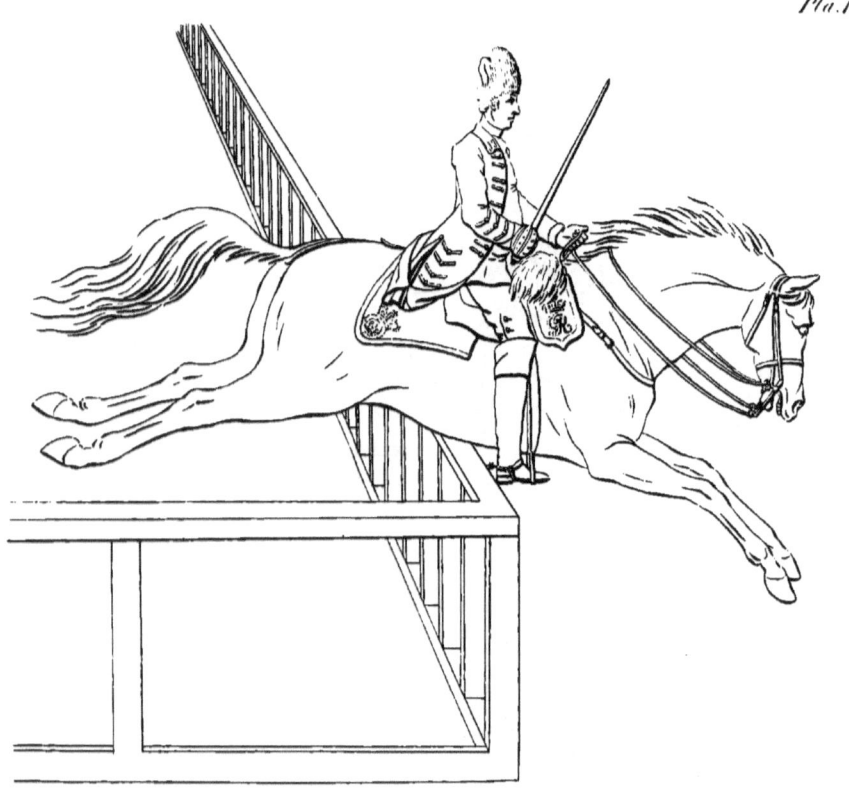

Pla.12.

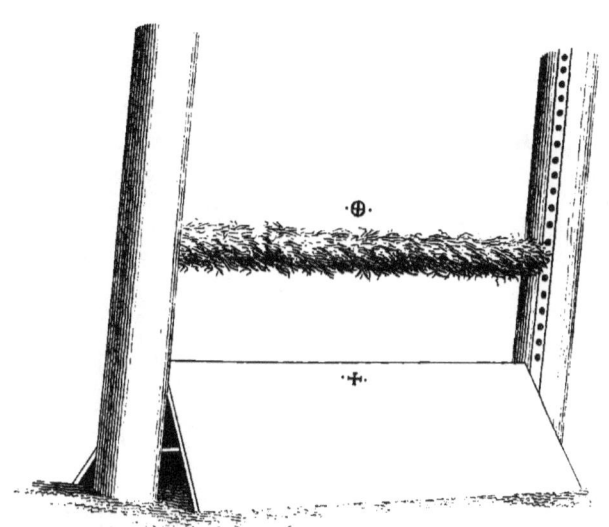

Pl. 16.

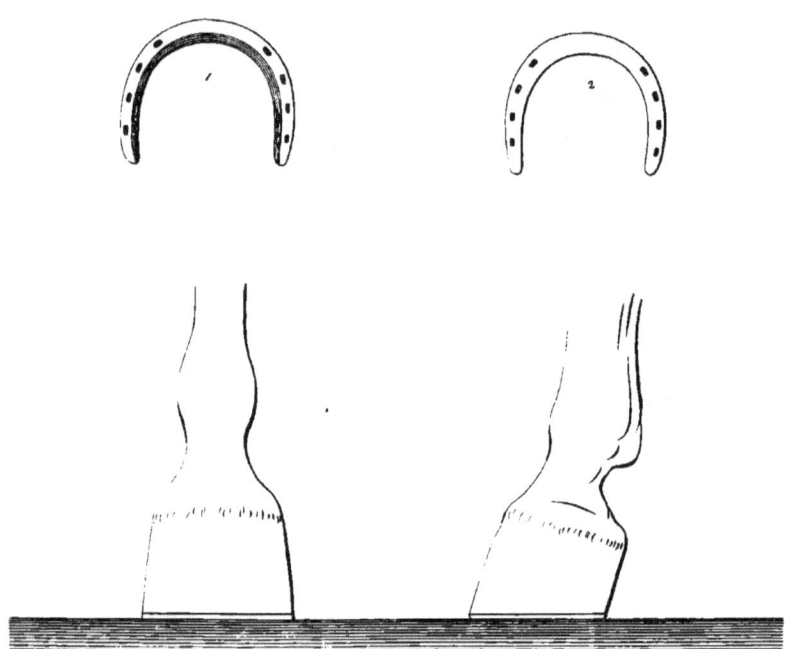

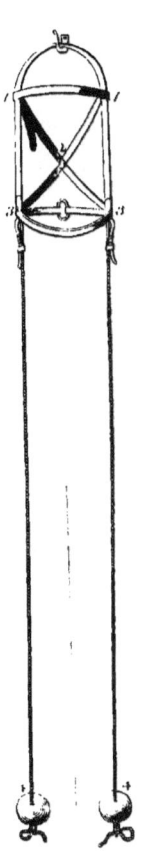

www.ingramcontent.com/pod-product-compliance
Lightning Source LLC
Chambersburg PA
CBHW020259170426
43202CB00008B/435